JONATHAN FREJUSTE

WHO TAUGHT YOU TO LOVE?

TOOLS FOR BUILDING BELONGING,
SAFE SPACES, AND A LIFE OF PURPOSE

Copyright © 2022 Jonathan Frejuste All rights reserved.

Scripture quotations marked NLT are taken from the Holy Bible, New Living Translation, copyright ©1996, 2004, 2007, 2013, 2015 by Tyndale House Foundation. Used by permission of Tyndale House Publishers, Inc., Carol Stream, Illinois 60188. All rights reserved.

Scripture quotations marked NIV are taken from THE HOLY BIBLE, NEW INTERNATIONAL VERSION®, NIV® Copyright © 1973, 1978, 1984, 2011 by Biblica, Inc.™ Used by permission. All rights reserved worldwide.

Scripture quotations marked (NKJV) are taken from the NEW KING JAMES VERSION®. Copyright© 1982 by Thomas Nelson, Inc. Used by permission. All rights reserved.

Scripture quotations marked (ISV) are taken from the INTERNATIONAL STANDARD VERSION, Copyright© 1996-2008 by the ISV Foundation. All rights reserved internationally.

Scripture quotations marked ERV are taken from the Holy Bible: Easy-to-Read Version (ERV), International Edition © 2013, 2016 by Bible League International and used by permission.

Scripture is taken from NOG, GOD'S WORD®, © 1995 God's Word to the Nations. Used by permission of Baker Publishing Group.

The Scriptures quoted are from the NET Bible® http://netbible.com copyright ©1996, 2019 used with permission from Biblical Studies Press, L.L.C. All rights reserved

Scripture quotations marked (NIrV) are taken from the Holy Bible, New International Reader's Version®, NIrV® Copyright © 1995, 1996, 1998, 2014 by Biblica, Inc.™ Used by permission of Zondervan. All rights reserved worldwide. www.zondervan.com The "NIrV" and "New International Reader's Version" are trademarks registered in the United States Patent and Trademark Office by Biblica, Inc.™

Scripture quotations marked (GNT) are from the Good News Translation in Today's English Version- Second Edition Copyright © 1992 by American Bible Society. Used by Permission.

Scripture quotations marked (TLB) are taken from The Living Bible copyright © 1971. Used by permission of Tyndale House Publishers, a Division of Tyndale House Ministries, Carol Stream, Illinois 60188. All rights reserved.

Scripture quotations marked NLV are taken from the New Life Version, copyright © 1969 and 2003. Used by permission of Barbour Publishing, Inc., Uhrichsville, Ohio 44683. All rights reserved.

Scripture quotations marked KJV from The Authorized (King James) Version. Rights in the Authorized Version in the United Kingdom are vested in the Crown. Reproduced by permission of the Crown's patentee, Cambridge University Press

Scripture quotations marked MSG are taken from THE MESSAGE, copyright © 1993, 1994, 1995, 1996, 2000, 2001, 2002 by Eugene H. Peterson. Used by permission of NavPress. All rights reserved. Represented by Tyndale House Publishers, Inc.

Scripture taken from The Voice™. Copyright © 2012 by Ecclesia Bible Society. Used by permission. All rights reserved.

Scripture quotations marked TPT are from The Passion Translation®. Copyright © 2017, 2018 by Passion & Fire Ministries, Inc. Used by permission. All rights reserved. thePassionTranslation.com.

Scripture quotations marked (CEV) are from the Contemporary English Version Copyright © 1991, 1992, 1995 by American Bible Society, Used by Permission.

Scripture quotations taken from the Amplified® Bible (AMPC), Copyright © 1954, 1958, 1962, 1964, 1965, 1987

Scripture taken from the International Children's Bible® (ICB). Copyright © 1986, 1988, 1999 by Thomas Nelson. Used by permission. All rights reserved.

Scripture quotations taken from the Amplified® Bible (AMP), Copyright © 2015 by The Lockman Foundation

Scripture taken from the SAINT JOSEPH NEW CATHOLIC BIBLE® (NCB) Copyright © 2019 by Catholic Book Publishing Corp. Used with permission. All rights reserved.

Scripture taken from The Expanded Bible. (EXB) Copyright ©2011 by Thomas Nelson. Used by permission. All rights reserved.

This book is designed to provide information and motivation to our readers. It is sold with the understanding that the author and the publisher is not engaged to render any type of psychological, legal, or any other kind of professional advice. The content of each article is the sole expression and opinion of its author. No warranties or guarantees are expressed or implied by the publisher's choice to include any of the content in this volume. Neither the publisher nor the individual author(s) shall be liable for any physical, psychological, emotional, financial, or commercial damages, including, but not limited to, special, incidental, consequential or other damages. Our views and rights are the same: You are responsible for your own choices, actions, and results.

Table of Contents

Introduction vii

Part 1: Safe People Create Belonging—*You Belong Here* 1
1   Find and Value Each Person's Voice in the Community 7
2   Clear Up Assumptions and Set Valid Expectations: Is
    The Story I'm Telling Myself True? 13
3   Do the Work: Understand Your Family Background 21
4   Listening without Agenda: The Greatest Superpower 31
5   Assertiveness: Speak Your Peace From the Inside Out 41
6   Clean Fighting: Words Can Bring Death or Life 49

Part 2: Safe Spaces Are Free of Chronic Tension and Anxiety—
You're Safe To Be Vulnerable 55
7   Forgiveness: The Cornerstone of Reconciliation 59
8   Grieving: Joy Comes In the Mourning 65
9   Shame and Judgment: Do You Want to Get Well Again? 73

Part 3: Safe Communities Launch People Into their Destinies—
You Have Purpose 115
10 Who Are You? and What Time Is It?: Know What Season
    of Life You're In 121
11 Mind Your Business: Find Your Lane, Run Your Own Race,
    and Let Your Light Shine 131
12 Friendship DRAFT: Have Standards/Radar for Choosing/
    Being Safe Friends 143

13	Dreams to Reality: Get a Vision or Perish	161
14	Develop a Code of Conduct: Log Out and Check Yourself So No One Has To	171
15	Sweat Equity: Put in the Work to Become an Emotionally Mature (Loving) Adult	179

Choosing a Counselor 183
What Is TheBridge330? 186
About the Author 189
End notes 191

Introduction

I was in the third grade, sitting at home with my mother while I did my homework, and she watched the news. As the news report flashed, I remember hearing that more than 800,000 people were murdered in the course of 100 days in a country called Rwanda. I looked at my mom in horror and disbelief, searching for confirmation that what I heard was as horrific as I thought. My mother also stared at the screen in disbelief at the atrocity.

I didn't know how to follow the story at the time. At such a young age, I didn't have the ability to understand its dynamics. Later as an adult, I revisited the story to learn its history and the stories of the survivors.

When I ask you who taught you to love, the people of Rwanda are certainly a force for good in learning the power of love, forgiveness, and reconciliation. After the genocide they endured, rather than pursuing retaliation, the next few years were spent promoting national unity and rebuilding the country's economy.

What is needed to repair a broken unity and trust in a relationship, especially in this case, is an unbelievable level of grace, mercy, and forgiveness. There's no doubt that healing is messy. Many of the survivors were children at the time and were adopted by family members. The consistent themes of the survivors focused on finding new places of belonging, safe places to process their pain, and making peace with the history in a way that unlocked their destiny. I believe this played a major role in healing the nation and contributing to the stability it has today.

We all benefit from using the tools of grace, the wisdom to implement them, and the patience to trust the process of building and healing. When a country is in chaos, everybody has a plan to fix it—but it takes a leader of real understanding to straighten things out (Proverbs 28:2, MSG).

A core philosophy of the TheBridge330 Mentoring Program is that we must **prepare for life's battles before the battles come**. We are to be proactive, preventative, and instructive instead of corrective, chastising, and punishing.

Loving relationships don't come from intention. They come from the application of knowing of how to love. The longer you accumulate relational experiences without having the right tools, the more tension, anxiety, misunderstandings, and invalid expectations you will feel.

I've had the privilege of learning from lived experience. The most immediate issues we must all face in life are loss, heartbreak, family tension, and breakdown. These include the lingering effects of child abuse, divorce, and domestic violence.

More than anything else, in light of the times we live in, people need more safety. In the following chapters I'll discuss safety from three perspectives:

1. Safe people create emotional security (a sense of belonging). Safe people say: **You belong here.**
2. Safe spaces are free of chronic tension and anxiety. Space spaces say: **It's safe for you to be vulnerable here.**
3. Safe communities foster opportunities for positive well-being and fulfillment. Safe communities say: **You have a purpose.**

Each section will help you develop skills, perspectives, and tools for your consideration and application.

A major word of caution: Pride and arrogance keep many people from progressing in life and relationships. "Knowledge produces arrogance" (1 Corinthians 8:1, MEV). Our pride and arrogance tell us we already have all the answers; this is false and can keep us from receiving life-changing information.

If there is something in this guide that you have a different perspective on, leave it be and take what you *do* resonate with. In other words, **chew the meat and spit out the bone.**

Let's start!

Part 1

Safe People Create Belonging—*You Belong Here*

I once spoke with a therapist who told me about her work with children who were dealing with behavioral disorders. She said that she stopped doing that work.

"Why?" I asked.

She replied, "The child would get better for two or three weeks and then become a terror again." She said she came to realize that if you don't also equip the people who live with the child, it doesn't matter how much you help the child. The child will become whatever the people in the environment allow her or him to be. She also made the very salient point that, regardless of income or education, *anyone* can be unhealthy/toxic.

This was a lightbulb moment for me! In my experience, most people (myself included) spend hours and hours preparing for our careers, but we don't spend time learning how to love well. The purpose of life is more than connecting—but it can't be achieved apart from connecting.

Why has a lifetime of education failed to educate us about healthy relationships?

The sad irony is that many intimate relationships are places where disrespect and contempt occur. People in these relationships get to know each other on a deeper, more authentic level—yet I've seen people treat acquaintances with more kindness and care than family, friends, and spouses.

Why do people sometimes treat those closest to them with contempt?

- Maybe it's because a close relationship is the one place where we can put our guard down without fear of being abandoned.
- Maybe it's because boundary violations have become normalized in intimate relationships.
- Maybe it's because we were not taught that relationships require intentionality and learning the skills to love well.
- Maybe it's because we can't *be* what we've never *seen*.

WHO TAUGHT YOU TO LOVE?

History has taught me that we, as people, rarely learn from history. It's time for that to change. It's time for us to become intentional about learning the skills to love well and create safety.

Without intentional focus on love, relational problems are bound to happen. These problems include poor listening, failed attempts at empathy, emotional distance, controlling behavior, broken commitments, and condemnation or judgment of the people we hold closest.

Most people were not raised in emotionally safe families. They are living with a legacy of pain from the childhood wounds. Now more than ever, people need safe relationships to heal their hearts and rewire their minds. We need to become accustomed to loving spaces instead of dysfunctional ones.

People who feel they are unloved and don't belong inevitably experience tremendous suffering. On the contrary, people who feel loved, accepted, and valued experience a feeling of being at home. But loving relationships require regular maintenance. When it comes to love, we need fewer emergency surgeries and more regular doctor visits.

In the first section, we'll walk through tools that we can use to foster trust and prevent relationship breakdown. If you're accustomed to being in families, friendships, and communities where loving relationships are not the highest priority—where slander, judgment, gossip, and disrespect have been normalized—these skills might feel difficult to apply.

It's important note that these tools also should be handled carefully. Just as fire can be used to warm food or to burn down a house, and a hammer can build a house or become a weapon, relationships can make people more vulnerable to the things you say and do. As you practice these skills, it's important to stay aware of your tone of voice and the intention of your heart.

Relationship skills can even feel uncomfortable and weird. This is totally normal. New skills are like training wheels. Be patient with yourself and keep trying. The skills are easier to understand than they are to implement. But like any skill, the more you practice it, the better you'll become. Soon, these new ways of thinking and acting will become second nature.

Let's start!

Levels of Emotional Safety

It is better to eat a dry crust of bread in peace and quiet than to eat a big dinner in a house full of fighting.
Proverbs 17:1, NIRV

I've participated in about 100 workshops over the course of a decade. I will tell you that most people fear the most is that they will be judged. When we feel judged, we cannot feel safe.

We all have the capacity to create safe and loving environments at home, in the classroom, and at the workplace—but are we in the habit of encouraging love, or are we more accustomed to judging each other?

When people don't realize their power, they can unintentionally create unhealthy or even toxic environments. How many parents are not aware of what's going on with their children emotionally? Their children might feel unsafe, and nobody in the household might know that. Even adults often don't realize how emotionally unsafe they feel in their relationships. I have been and can be guilty of that.

As the Scripture above alludes to, it's better to be alone than in a toxic environment. It can be dangerous to be open and vulnerable around people who are hurting us.

Here are few things to reflect on and consider.

Emotionally Violent Spaces

In this kind of environment, there is no listening at the heart level. Listening takes place only for gathering information that is later used in manipulative ways. People keep secrets out of fear that their experiences and perspectives will be invalidated, held in contempt, or manipulated to hurt them. People in emotionally violent spaces feel a constant sense that they are being judged and will be judged. Differences in opinions result in being cut off or worse, as there is no room for ambiguity. Disagreements are handled in inappropriate and toxic ways. There is a chronic disregard for and violation of boundaries. Verbal abuse goes unchecked, along with backstabbing, exploitation, and recklessness. The concept of self-reflection is scoffed at. There is no self-accountability—only attacks on others for perceived problems. The emotional lives of people who live in emotionally violent places are severely damaged. Their expectations of others might be inappropriate, and they might become violent when their needs are unmet. They live with a constant sense of danger.

Emotionally Unhealthy Spaces

In an emotionally unhealthy space, listening is done for the purpose of rebuttals instead of truly connecting. Persistent conflicts and problems are managed by avoidance and by tactics like cutting people off, speaking in absolutes, changing the subject, overstating the case, and controlling the conversation using directive questions. People in emotionally unhealthy environments refuse to engage in self-reflection regarding interpersonal relationship problems. Boundaries are never clearly communicated and remain perpetually blurry. Emotional closeness can't be achieved due to the lack of trust. In this setting, peoples' emotional lives are bottled up. Differences in opinions result in avoidance and surface-level resolution. Expectations of others are not communicated clearly and at times, they are unrealistic or not agreed upon. Maintaining the status quo is more important than ensuring that everyone feels and knows they are loved.

Emotionally Safe Spaces

In an emotionally safe space, listening is done at the heart level while each person retains their individuality. Each person has permission to appropriately share their thoughts, feelings, and experiences in a way that doesn't undermine or invalidate the experience of others. Self-reflection is a mainstay in the community dynamic, so there are fewer triggering interactions. Boundaries are clearly communicated and firmly established. Problems are resolved personally, privately, and peacefully using "clean" fighting techniques. Difficult conversations are conducted clearly, respectfully, and honestly. When confusion is experienced, it is investigated maturely, without jumping to conclusions. There is flexibility around the rules when the situation calls for a wise revision. Family members sometimes experience real delight and feelings of love and trust. There is a good capacity for growth in intimacy and a strong sense of security and trust. When a difference of opinion happens, people can work through it while respecting the alternative viewpoint.

Your Work

Which emotional space level described above represents the manner in which you were raised?

Which level represents the way you operate now in your close relationships?

What kind of emotional space do you feel would be most conducive to your well-being and the well-being of others?

— 1 —

Find and Value Each Person's Voice in the Community

Through [skillful and godly] wisdom a house [a life, a home, a family] is built, And by understanding it is established [on a sound and good foundation].
Proverbs 23:4, AMP

Building healthy communities where people's voices are heard and valued is not going to happen by intention. It begins with relationships that have become emotionally safe spaces where people are heard and valued.

In relationships, closeness is a measure of affection. Relationships grow close through the investment of trust, positive exchanges, and a subsequent accumulation of positive experiences. Our communities can grow when supplied with the same elements.

Often, it's not what happens to us that forms us—it's what *should have happened* but did not. If we want to bring about relational health, we have to give time and attention to the aspects and impacts of emotional safety. Emotional health is especially important in our relationships, so that we can manufacture quality memories with one another. Even if the time we have is limited, we can manufacture quality moments, so we have great things to reflect on. Good memories have a positive effect on health and well-being.

The following exercises are called Community Temperature Reading.[1] This analysis is a way to assess most of the conversations in your community, on a scale of negative to positive.

Conversations are used to express appreciation, resolve light conflicts, share new information, make requests, and share hopes and dreams. In a positive relationship, both sides contribute ideas and both are receptive to listening to the other person.

This tool was designed to honor each person's God-given and unique personality and temperament. The best thing we can do for anyone is to help them find their God-given voice.

If you've never done this kind of exercise, it might feel strange. Imagine riding a bicycle for the first time at fifty years old with training wheels—weird and uncomfortable! The key is sticking with it.

Why do we need these exercises?

1. Appreciations
This exercise is used to share heartfelt expressions of gratitude.

- We might think of how grateful we feel, but we don't regularly make it a point to share this. It usually is only shared when someone has gone far above and beyond the call of duty.
- Some families and cultures rarely express their gratitude—but appreciation is vital to the life of any relationship or community.
- You find what you look for. Think of ways you can express your appreciation for the little things people do every day in order to build a habit of finding and accentuating the good in and from others.

Examples of appreciations:
"I appreciate that you waited for me the other day when I was running late."
"I appreciate you arriving early and getting everything ready before the meeting."

2. Puzzles: Because You Can't Be Angry and Curious at the Same Time.
This exercise is used to get you to be curious instead of making assumptions.

- When you don't understand something, it's a puzzle. Using the word "puzzle" keeps you from making negative interpretations of people's actions, especially when situations are unclear.
- "Don't jump to conclusions—there may be a perfectly good explanation for what you just saw" (Proverbs 25:8, MSG).
- "Do not judge and criticize and condemn [others unfairly with an attitude of self-righteous superiority as though assuming the office of a judge], so that you will not be judged [unfairly]" (Matthew 7:1, AMP). This advice keeps you from being judgmental.

Examples of considering the unknown as a puzzle:
Shift your emphasis from expressing anger based on an assumption to finding out more information. Instead of angrily saying, "You didn't call me back," you can say, "I'm puzzled as to why you didn't call me back."

Instead of thinking, *No one cleaned up after the party. I live with slobs!* You can say, "I wonder why they didn't clean up after the party."

3. Complaints with a Suggested Solution
This exercise allows you to validate your grievances about annoyances and small irritations without attacking the other person's character. Healthy communication is the freedom to **express our wants and needs without demanding.**

In a relationship, there will be things you don't like. You might have a complaint that you want to bring forward. But the manner in which you find resolution matters immensely, because it affects building trust and preventing relationship breakdown.

Many of our families have conditioned us to either not say anything unless you have something nice to say or to confront in a manner that is unhealthy and disrespectful.

Many people bring forward grievances without any responsibility for a solution.

Examples of complaining *with* a suggested solution:
Use the format: "I notice… and I would like to request…"

"I notice you often leave the lights on downstairs all night. I prefer that the downstairs be dark, so please turn off all the lights before you go to bed."

"I notice that you come to our meetings late, and I prefer starting at the agreed-upon time, so I'd like to ask that you arrive on time."

The person making the complaint should take some responsibility for coming up with a possible solution.

Always keep your complaints respectful and *light* during this exercise.

4. Life Update
This exercise is used to share personal, intimate information about oneself. One of the biggest challenges in relationships is that, as people grow into their unique selves, their ideologies, desires, and plans for life begin to shift—but none of us has a real blueprint to share these changes with those we love.

We need to learn a way to share when we have *news*—which can mean opportunities, events, new decisions, appointments, achievements, or activities. Relationships grow when people know what is occurring in each other's lives. This includes the trivial as well as the important things.

Examples of providing a life update:
"I've decided to go back to school. I've already applied to a few schools."
"The doctor says my cholesterol level is fine."
"We're moving out next week. We just closed on our first house."

1. Hopes and Dreams
This exercise is used to share desires for our future in relationships and in life in general.

- Our hopes and wishes reveal to others the uniqueness of our souls and the most important parts of who we are.
- Our relationships become richer as we support and listen to each other's hopes and dreams.
- We should have the courage to let those we love know which things are most important in the big picture of our lives.

Activity with a Partner
To get started with these tools, complete these sentences:

> I appreciate……
> I'm puzzled by …
> I notice … and I would like to request……
> My new information is….
> I hope …

Pair up with a partner and read through the guidelines for the Community Temperature Reading.

- Think about what kinds of conversations you hear the most in your community and how these conversations also happen in your life and the lives of those close to you.
- Face each other as you speak.
- Take turns sharing, back and forth, as you use the sentence stems.
- Keep sharing brief and light.
- Don't respond or interrupt. Only respond to complaints or puzzles with a few words, and work on one category at a time.
- Use one exercise at a time.

Small Group Sharing[2]
In building emotionally safe communities, we have to risk intimate emotional contact. Sometimes, healthy ways of relating conflict with people's cultures and family rules. This tool can be used with children and families, at the workplace, with friends, or in classrooms. Because communication is also about what's being heard, pay attention to the reactions and interpretations you see.

In groups of three or four, think back to the way you grew up and answer the following questions:

1. How did your family of origin express appreciation? Hopes and wishes? Complaints?
2. What was it like for you to express yourself in these different categories?
3. Which was easiest for you? Which was most difficult for you?

Final question: Of everything you just said, what's the most important thing you would like me to remember?

Things to Remember about Emotional Safety Exercises:

- They are meant to be tools, not weapons.
- They can be used one-on-one or in a group setting.
- You can use them with friends, family, in classrooms, or in a small group.
- If time is limited, you can choose just one or two exercises to use.

Conclusion

One of the most painful feelings is being misunderstood or not heard. The root of a lot of conflict is that what is important to one person might not be important to the other person. With this set of exercises, you have a scaffolding to find your voice and allow other people to learn who you are and what you need. You will also develop the framework to learn about them at a deeper level.

— 2 —

Clear Up Assumptions and Set Valid Expectations: Is The Story I'm Telling Myself True?[3]

The greatest nation is the imagination.

Chadwick Boseman starred in the 2020 film *Da 5 Bloods* alongside Clarke Peters, an actor he referred to as one of his idols. In an interview shortly after Boseman's passing from his unpublicized battle with colon cancer, Peters talked about their friendship. He admitted that when his wife asked him about his co-star, he had described Boseman as a person who had an exaggerated sense of self-importance, possibly due to the record-breaking success of the culture-shifting movie *Black Panther*. In tears, Peters acknowledged that he had misjudged Boseman. Boseman's cancer had caused him tremendous pain and he needed special care, which others on the set noticed and interpreted as a bourgeoisie need for pampering.

People often make assumptions without ever attempting to verify the facts. Sadly, they sometimes then pass around those assumptions in the form of gossip, which can damage relationships and cause further confusion and conflict. Getting information to replace your assumptions can be uncomfortable, but the maturity of any relationship can be measured by your ability to have uncomfortable conversations.

Let's look at some scenarios.

Common scenarios where people "mind read" instead of getting information:

- You call someone, and they don't pick up.
- A coworker sounds irritated at your question.
- Someone walks past and doesn't acknowledge you.

These situations are common, but sadly, some have caused tremendous damage to relationships simply because people misunderstood and then responded inappropriately.

Some common assumptions or "mind readings" conclusions:

- They must be mad at me.
- I sounded dumb. I should have known the answer.
- They must think I'm not that important.

While these assumptions might be true, they are certainly worth having a conversation about, if you value the relationship. Expecting people to read your mind is both unrealistic and unfair.

As a mature and loving person who is "ready to believe the best of every person" (1 Cor. 13:7, AMPC), be the one to take responsibility and learn the real explanation.

Here are actual scenarios that I've experienced personally or heard firsthand accounts of. Think about these situations when you're tempted to assume you know why someone behaved rudely or indifferently to you:

- "I'm sorry Jon. My wife went into labor." (This one really happened to me!)
- "I just got some distressing news."
- "My mom just died, and I feel so zoned out."

Exercise: Stop Mind Reading

This exercise is about clearing up assumptions and verifying facts in order to prevent relationship breakdown.

Important Note:

We must never assume that we know what someone else is thinking or feeling, because we might tell ourselves things that aren't true.

Individual Activity

1. Think about the different relationships in your life—with your family (marriage, children, parents, siblings, extended family), friendships, neighbors, roommates, or coworkers
2. Choose a situation where you might be "mind reading" or making up a story to explain someone's behavior.

Partner Activity
Ask one person in the group to play the role of the person you chose, and then practice this skill.

1. First ask:
    - "Do I have permission to read your mind?" or
    - "Can I check out a story I have been telling myself?"
2. After the person answers yes:
    - Ask how they feel toward you. "I think that you believe (something about me) … Is this true?" An example might be, "I think that you believe I'm the boss' favorite" or "I think you consider me too young for this job." Listen carefully to their response.
    - Ask about a specific incident. "I am curious. When you (their behavior), were you upset with me?" Example: "When you failed to answer my text, were you upset with me?" or "When you snapped at me yesterday, was it because of something I said?"

The responses you receive will give you different possible interpretations of why someone acted as they did and how they feel about you. You might be surprised at how much you have "mind read" into a simple act.

Reflection: Wisdom vs. Foolishness

As we get older, we should get wiser and avoid making assumptions without verifying the facts in our relationships and in life in general. Scripture from the book of Proverbs provides insight on showing restraint about making assumptions.

> *Don't jump to conclusions—there may be a perfectly good explanation for what you just saw.*
> Proverbs 25:8, MSG

> *He who answers before he hears [the facts]— It is folly and shame to him.*
> Proverbs 18:13, AMP

Wise people want to learn more, so they listen closely to gain knowledge.
Proverbs 18:15, ERV

A fool takes no pleasure in understanding but only in disclosing what is on his mind.
Proverbs 18:2, NET

Based on the above Proverbs, what are the differences between a foolish person and a wise person?

Reflection: Get All Sides the Story

The first person to tell his side of a story seems right. But that may change when somebody comes and asks him questions.
Proverbs 18:17, ICB

Think of a recent scenario where you had an expectation of someone and they let you down. What story did you tell yourself about why that happened? Take time to think of the story and how long you held on to it. Do you believe you understood the real explanation? What else might have happened?

Expectations

The worst disappointments are not caused by what you find, but by what you *expected* to find. Unmet expectations cause most of our frustrations.

But sometimes, our expectations are invalid. Just because we have expectations doesn't mean that we have a right to them. We need to consider whether our expectations are fair and reasonable. Expectations come from a variety of places: school, church, TV/ movies, family, friends, etc. Your expectations might be unspoken, and you might have no awareness of them until they are unmet—and by that point, anger or disappointment have moved in.

Remember: Your anger and disappointment are unwarranted if the expectations were not valid in the first place. So what makes an expectation valid?

A valid expectation has four traits (which form the acronym CARS):

C – Conscious: There's an awareness of the expectation by both parties.
A – Agreed Upon: Both parties agree to the expectation.
R – Realistic: The people involved have the ability and willingness to meet the expectation.
S – Spoken: There has been a clear expression of the expectation.

Unrealistic expectations cause confusion everywhere we go. The violation of expectations can lead to broken relationships in marriages, families, and businesses. Certain events seem fraught with expectations. Holidays are especially problematic, but so are vacations, family functions, date nights, birthdays, household chores, and weddings. We expect certain things to happen and certain behavior from those around us, as dictated by the event itself.

Think about what you expect from the people around you. Use the list to go through your expectations and decide whether they are valid. Does everyone know what you expect and do they have the ability to do what you expect? Have you asked them clearly to do what you expect?

Albert Einstein said that the most incomprehensible aspect about the universe is that it is comprehensible. I believe that is also true about relationships. Many problems in relationships are preventable if we take the time to understand and manage our expectations. Unspoken agreements or expectations have the greatest potential to cause trouble.

I believe you can prevent half of the drama in relationships by bringing your expectations to the light. You can't be angry and curious at the same time.

Note: The words "They should know" come from the pit of hell. Nothing destroys a relationship quicker than the mindset that the people in your life should already know what you believe, think, feel, or expect without you informing them.

Key principle: An expectation is only valid when it is mutually agreed upon. An exception to this key principle are the expectations between a parent and child (e.g., expected chores, courtesy), but even these should be discussed and agreed upon when the child is old enough to understand. Be aware that you might have already agreed to certain expectations in your work contracts and marriage vows.

Individual Activity
Exercise: Go through a recent, simple expectation you had that went unmet, which made you upset or frustrated. Maybe you didn't get a birthday card, or someone didn't return your text, or someone forgot to take out the trash. Ask yourself ...

>**Conscious** – Were you aware that you had the expectation?
>**Agreed Upon** – Did the other person agree to the expectation?
>**Realistic** – Was your expectation reasonable? What evidence did you have that this person could or would do this?
>**Spoken** – Did you clearly express the expectation—or did you just think "they should've known?"

Partner Activity
Exercise: Use a partner to practice saying these statements, which can help you clarify expectations and assumptions:

- "I'd like to clarify an expectation I have of you. Is this a valid expectation?"
- "I expect (your action) ... because (the situation.) Can we agree to that?"
- "Can I check out an assumption I have of you? Is this true?"

Some examples of these statements in real life:

- "I'd like to clarify an expectation I have of you. I expect you to call me on my birthday and get me a gift or at least a card. Is this a valid expectation?"
- "I expect you to fill up my tank when you borrow my car, because I would do that for you. Can we agree to that?"
- "Can I check out an assumption I have of you? I'm assuming that you didn't respond to my text because of the argument we had … is this true?"

Two Common Questions

1. What do I do when someone is unable to meet my expectation?
2. What do I do if I have an agreed-upon expectation with someone and they don't do it?

– 3 –

DO THE WORK: UNDERSTAND YOUR FAMILY BACKGROUND

"Jesus is in your heart, but grandpa is in your bones."
Pastor Pete Scazzero

Your family of origin is the most powerful group to which you will ever belong. They become part of your makeup and wiring as a person. A family creates a map for life. It's as if we are all born with an unformatted disk in our hearts and souls. Our family writes the programming to tell us how life should go and how to respond. They also show us how to relate to others and form our values.

Sometimes, your family's lessons are spoken and other times, unspoken. As you grow older, you realize that more is *caught* than *taught*. People may look like players acting alone, but they are larger players in a system that goes back generations. Unfortunately, many families and cultures are more committed to their scripts than to actually changing negative legacies in order to support a more positive future.

Human nature conditions us to stay with what's familiar, even if it's unhealthy. We fear the unknown and we'd rather not venture there. Unlearning wrong ideas and relearning truths about ourselves in order to change our programming for the better is a difficult process. We often hold beliefs, values, and assumptions that we have never examined. One of the best ways to start changing this is cultivating a level of awareness about your own beliefs.

Exercise 1 (Reflection): How would you describe the family atmosphere you grew up in? Try to use just a word or two (ex.: affirming, complaining, critical, approachable, angry, tense, cooperative, close, distant, fun, serious).

_____

_____

Exercise 2: What messages and scripts has your family passed down to you?

Below is an exercise to get a sense of what scripts and messages your upbringing gave you. Family patterns from the past can show up in our present relationships, often without us being aware of it. Most of us never examine the scripts handed to us by our past.

As we grow older, we recognize the depths of the influence of those who raised us and how their messages affect our behavior and self-esteem. As children, we may have seen or experienced things that intuitively struck us as inappropriate or wrong. But because we were children, our perceptions might have been dismissed as naïve or uninformed.

As a result, many children think that something must be wrong with the way they see things—or even that something is wrong with them. Let's take an assessment to identify the scripts/messages you've been given. Take your time when reviewing this questionnaire. Don't feel rushed. Approach this exercise with patience and reflection.

These are sample messages some of us got from our families:

1. **Family**: "Family interactions involve fear, obligation, and guilt instead of love, respect, and independence. (My family planted seeds of this message in me). You owe your family until you die. You have a duty to family and culture that supersedes everything else. Never share your family's dirty laundry, even if unhealthy and/or abusive things are taking place in the family."
2. **Emotions**: "Feelings are not important. You are not allowed to have feelings. You can react based on how you feel without processing your emotions."
3. **Attitudes about culture**: "Don't have friends from outside of your culture. Our culture is better than other cultures. Don't marry someone from outside your culture."
4. **Money**: "There is never enough money. Every penny we make has to be spent on something before the next money arrives. It's okay to borrow money that you might never be able to repay. If your needs cost money, they are putting a strain on the family budget."
5. **Anger**: "Don't show your anger. Anger is a bad and dangerous thing. Sarcasm is a way to show anger. It's appropriate to explode in anger to make a point."
6. **Relationships**: "Relationships are dangerous. Don't trust anyone. People will hurt you. Never let yourself be vulnerable."

7. **Grief and sadness**: "You're not allowed to feel bad. Sadness is a sign of weakness. Don't be depressed. You need to get over losses quickly."
8. **Conflict**: "You are not allowed to respectfully disagree. Avoid conflict at all costs. Loud, angry, constant fighting is normal. Physical altercations are prime options to resolve a conflict."
9. **Sex**: "It's wrong and dangerous. Don't talk about sex. Men can be promiscuous, but women have to be chaste. Women are only worthy of love if they are worthy of sexual desire."
10. **Success**: "Nothing matters more. You have to get into the best schools and make a lot of money. Your wealth is a measure of who you are. You can't be a success until you get married and have kids."

Sample scripts and their underlying messages

- You exist to keep everybody else happy.
- You don't have a right to enjoy your life.
- It's not okay to make mistakes.
- Your worth and value is based on what you do, not who you are.
- No matter what happens, don't embarrass the family. Make us look good in public.
- Don't trust your intuition. Trust what we tell you.
- Don't assert yourself. Submit to our authority.
- Don't tell. Keep our family secrets.
- Always be nice.
- Don't feel what you feel.
- Don't trust people outside your family, neighborhood, or culture.
- Don't trust yourself to manage your own sexuality.
- Keep smiling, no matter what.
- Don't ask questions.
- Don't tell us how you feel. You don't have a right to your own opinion.

Do any of these scripts or messages resonate with you? Can you add to this list? This might be the first time you have taken a deeper look at the scripts your family handed you. Rest assured that this list places all people on level ground These messages can be found in every age, race, and culture.

This exercise can be divisive, but also uniting. Nobody comes from a perfect family. This exercise exposes the issues and negative legacies common to all cultures. We all want to be perfect but know that we fall short.

The point of this assessment is to make you aware of ways that these legacies might have shaped you and point out where you might need to heal, grow, or change. Family messages die hard and can be very subtle. As much as this journey is about learning, it's also about *unlearning* everything that isn't healthy. Then you can be who you were meant to be in the first place.

See Chapter 7—Differentiation in ***Bridge the Gaps—Lessons on Self-Awareness, Self-Development, and Self-Care***. Go to www.thebridge330.com to pick up a copy.

Exercise 3: What type of family did you come from?

Family relationships can be sources of strength or systems of dysfunction. A parent's choices, fortunately or unfortunately, can decide life for everyone else. Poor choices lead to ways of operating that don't serve a healthy family life and emotional well-being.

You are responsible for your choices in your adult life, but your emotions were shaped by what your parents or guardians did and didn't do. Unfortunately, as children, we didn't have the emotional wisdom and maturity to recognize if the environment we were raised in was toxic. So in order to get along, we just went along.

As an adult and mentor, take some time to identify the level of family health you experienced during your upbringing. Here's a framework of family health. Think about where your family of origin would fall in this framework.

Family Health Levels

Level 5 —Severely troubled family. This a confused family where there is no clear leadership, no clarity or coherence, and a constant sense of danger. It's full of unresolved conflicts and ungrieved losses, similar to a picture of a nation at war with itself.

Level 4 —Dictatorship. Instead of anarchy, there is a rigid system of rules enforced by intimidation and threats. Financial abuse is a common form of control. There is no room for diverse perspectives and no patience with ambiguity. The perceptions are black and white.

Level 3 —Average. At this level, there is no chaos or dictatorship, but the rules of the family are seen as more important than the people. You must follow the rules in order to feel loved. The words "should" and "ought" best define the family. People's emotional lives must be bottled up for the good of all. The chance of true emotional intimacy between one another is limited at this level.

Level 2 —Suitable. At this level, there is flexibility around the rules when the situation calls for a wise revision. Family members sometimes experience real delight and feelings of love and trust. There is a good capacity for growth in intimacy.

Level 1 —This level is similar to Level 2, but to a greater degree. There is a strong sense of security and trust. If a difference of perspective arises, there is either a strong chance that it can be worked out or that the alternative viewpoint will be respected.

What level was your family? Who made the rules, and what were the consequences of not following them? What can you add to the description for your family's level?

_____

_____

How did your family handle important decisions that needed to be made? How did your family adjust to change?

_____

_____

Family Pathologies

It's been said that a family is where a life makes up its mind. Patterns of sin and brokenness can be transmitted through the generations. To change, you must identify the sins of the family, because when you can see the patterns, you can then make a conscious decision to interrupt or break away from those patterns.

We shouldn't disrespect or betray our parents, but we need to see them objectively. Just because you love your family doesn't mean you have to be like them.

My time on this Earth has taught me that sometimes life is not fair. Sometimes we reap what we have not sown. You may not have created the problem, but it's yours to heal.

It can be helpful to identify what we call generational patterns and "earthquake" events.

- **Generational patterns** are incidents that tend to recur throughout the generations. You can decide to follow the pattern, or decide you will not follow it.
- **"Earthquake" events** are usually one-time, extremely disruptive incidents that change family life.

Generational themes of families: Out-of-wedlock birth, affairs, sexual abuse, alcoholism, workaholism, divorce, abortions, addictions, unstable marriages, enmeshment (overly close relationships), emotional abuse, financial instability, teenage pregnancy, untreated mental illness, domestic violence, incarceration, and drug abuse.

"Earthquake" events that affect families: Premature death, acts of crime or violence against a family member, suicide, war, cancer, business collapse, infidelity, natural disasters, or moving to another country.

Consider these lists. Which of these apply to your family of origin? What are some insights regarding how your family was impacted and how this has affected who you are today? What reflections and resolutions do you have from experiencing events on the lists above?

Examples of Reflections and Resolutions on generational themes and "earthquakes":

- I saw that the men in my family did not stay faithful to their wives, so I will stay faithful to mine.
- My father and grandfather were alcoholics, so I know I need to stay away from alcohol.
- My family has generations of out-of-wedlock births. It hasn't turned out well for us.
- My parent's addiction decided life for all of us. I'm going to be a better father to my daughter, so she doesn't go through what I went through.
- I don't want my son to have a father who is still broken in some areas because of childhood sexual abuse. I'm going to start going to counseling.
- I am my father's son, but not my father's choices. The cycle of incarceration ends with me.
- I'm not doing myself or my future family any favors by keeping secrets.

Some of us have become stuck in our family's value system and way of relating. You often have to re-organize your life to break cycles and root out deeply ingrained family patterns. The process might prove more difficult than you expect.

In many ways, dealing with family themes, scripts, and resolutions is a continual process. Life will always throw new challenges at us; often, they expose the values and ways of relating we picked up from our family background, including some that need to change. An important part of this exercise is determining what newfound realizations you have made.

Here's a statement that you might use in your group or even in your own personal time of reflection.

Reflection Questions

1. What are you beginning to realize? What do you now recognize about your family that you didn't recognize as a child?
2. In light of this exercise, what is one step that you can take to change harmful or negative generational patterns that have affected your life?

WHO TAUGHT YOU TO LOVE?

Examples of Responses

- I am beginning to realize that changing these family patterns is like getting off crack cocaine. Breaking deeply rooted family patterns might prove to be one of the most difficult tasks of my life.
- I am beginning to realize that real peace is not the same as living in stable misery.
- I am beginning to realize that the baggage of our families continues to shape us, even after we've left the house.
- I am beginning to realize that it's not only about changing who you are in front of people, but changing the depth of who you are.
- I am beginning to realize that some demons are inherited. Others are invited.
- I am beginning to realize that when you hear the voices that say, "You are going to be just like your mom or dad," you have to talk back.
- I am beginning to realize that if you don't deal with your stuff, your stuff will deal with you.
- I am beginning to realize that truth and freedom go hand in hand; if you're not living in truth, then you're not free.
- I am beginning to realize that if I do my work, I can help others do theirs.
- I am beginning to realize that I was too indoctrinated with my family's script to examine contradictory paradigms that might have been better for me.
- I am beginning to realize that I didn't create the problem, but it's mine to heal.
- I am beginning to realize that my biological family of origin does not determine my future; God does.
- I am beginning to realize that to see your drama clearly is to begin to free yourself from it.
- I am beginning to realize that I can build on the positive legacies and heal the negative ones.

Practical Next Steps

- Pick up information on family backgrounds and how they affect us. I suggest *Unlocking Your Family Patterns: Finding Freedom from a Hurtful Past* by Dr. Henry Cloud, Dave Carder, Dr. John Townsend, and Dr. Earl Henslin; and *The Genogram Journey: Reconnecting with Your Family* by Monica McGoldrick.
- Start a small group based around Part 1 (Self-Awareness) and Chapters 31 to 35 of **Bridge the Gaps. (www.thebridge330.com).**
- Find a therapist. Some of us require specific, skilled help to overcome the issues discussed above. See the *Choosing a Counselor* section at the end of the book.

— 4 —

Listening without Agenda: The Greatest Superpower

A family that doesn't know how to listen to one another will eventually be a group of people who have nothing left to say.

A major cause of human problems is how people behave when we strongly disagree. When emotions and stakes run high, people often revert to an unhealthy type of conversation. Most of us have not learned healthy ways to disagree.

In next two chapters, we'll discuss how to identify your values and resolve conflicts through negotiation or "clean fighting." Our goal is to learn how to stop unhealthy behaviors like silent treatment, sarcasm, passive aggressiveness, hitting, etc. While learning how to negotiate is important, we must first learn how to *listen*—not for the purpose of responding, but so we can truly understand a message someone is communicating and the heart behind the message.

Listening at the heart level—without making judgment or assumptions—is a mark of maturity and a vital step in building communities that can heal the wounds of the past and bring about true reconciliation. We need to hear the stories of those who share a different perspective. We need to practice *incarnational listening*—listening from the heart and trying to become fully immersed in the perspective of the speaker.

The goal of effective listening without agenda is not agreement or winning a competition. It is understanding without making judgments or assumptions about the person. Another way to look at listening without agenda is that it's like playing charades, not playing chess. Chess is about the next move. Charades is getting attuned to what someone is saying and the heart behind their message.

I'm under no illusion that this practice is easy. To some, it might even sound ridiculous. But I believe this is one of the most important lessons in this guide. In our society, we suffer from an inability to love, and one of the best ways to show love is to listen. Until you sit down and hear someone's story, you are not qualified to judge their situation.

Most people, myself included, come from families where we were never truly listened to, nor were we taught how to listen at the heart level. I know that when I wasn't listened to, I felt unloved, unwanted, and dismissed. This kept me from wanting to be close or share anything with others, because I knew that what I conveyed would not be valued.

As I'm writing this, the headlines are full of hot button issues like race, class, sexuality, gender equality, and religion. Unfortunately, they are revealing how poorly we handle disagreements. Some conversations require a certain level of character, internal stability, and emotional maturity. Otherwise, tackling these issues leads to consistent relational breakdown and a festering resentment.

This lack of civility breeds defensiveness and creates an environment that feels unsafe. This kills the hope for unity and reconciliation. When people don't feel safe, the conversation loses its genuineness and ultimately, its ability to affect change in a positive way. It's hard to change the way you speak to and listen to others, particularly if you've grown accustomed to having conversations that are contentious. We have to humbly ask ourselves: Has the way we've done things been effective in building strong communities, where people can have disagreements without being disagreeable?

Our goal is a community that fosters love, healing, safety, and truth through listening, which is the currency of community. It's impossible to incarnationally listen to someone without being changed. Listening is the most important part of a crucial dialogue. We have to always remember our purpose as we engage in conversations. Let's roll up our sleeves and get to work.

The goal of this exercise is to help you evaluate your maturity level.

Exercise—Listening Test: What are the ways you interact in conversation?[4]

Directions: Circle all the statements you can affirm.

1. My close friends would describe me as a responsive listener.
2. When people are upset with me, I am able to listen to them without being defensive.
3. I listen not only to the words people say but also to the feelings behind their words.
4. I have little interest in judging other people or quickly giving my opinion to them.
5. I am able to validate another person's feelings with empathy.
6. I am aware of my defensive tactics in stressful conversations (e.g. appeasing, ignoring, blaming, distracting).

7. I understand how the family I was raised in has shaped my present listening style.
8. I ask for clarification when listening rather than "filling in the blanks" with assumptions.
9. I don't interrupt or raise my voice to get my point across when another is speaking.
10. I give people my undivided attention when they are talking to me.
11. I don't overemphasize facts to promote my agenda.
12. I don't change the subject to avoid acknowledging my ignorance or my wrong information.
13. I acknowledge when I don't have enough information and need to research and reflect to have an informed answer.
14. I invite dialogue instead of debate. Dialogue encourages a free flow of information, while debate is about defending your position, with no desire to consider if the other side's perspective has some value. The desire to win drives us away from healthy dialogue because we point out flaws in the other person's argument instead of looking for value.

If you circled ten to fourteen statements, you are an outstanding listener. If you circled six to nine, you are very good; and four to five, good. If you circled three or fewer statements, you are a poor listener and might be in trouble trying to work things out through discussion. If you want to be really brave, after you score yourself, ask someone close to you to honestly rate you as a listener. Be grateful for the insight you receive from this exercise, and if necessary, decide to improve your listening skills.

In families, friendships, marriages, and communities in general, if people aren't being heard, they are developing an emotional guardedness that breeds a dysfunctional and even toxic environment. Relationships don't stand a good chance when there are repeated failures of empathy and understanding. Poor listening breaks up marriages, churches, businesses, and friendships. I heard one marriage counselor say that when a married couple stops listening to one another, they will have to listen to the therapist—and if that doesn't work, they will have to listen to the divorce lawyer, or ultimately to the judge who helps divide their assets. This comment painted a sobering picture of the importance of listening.

When we don't discuss serious topics, they become "the elephants in the room." Elephants grow as they feed on avoidance. If we are to move forward as a community, and even as a family, we need to have these conversations and work hard to listen to and understand one another.

Can listening really make a difference?

Listening helps us develop empathy and compassion for one another, which changes our perceptions and the decisions we make based on those perceptions. Finding a way to discuss our differences will determine our future as a people, because true listening creates the environment that breeds change. We might never achieve agreement across the board, but we can find a greater sense of compassion and a reduced sense of superiority. "I am right, and you are wrong" conversations don't lead to unity. Instead, they breed shame, hatred, and increased division.

I've participated in several support groups over the years where we were asked, at the first meeting, to write down our fears about being in the group. The majority of the people in every group said they feared being judged. No one wants to be judged. No one wants to have their deepest beliefs, thoughts, vulnerabilities, and pain dismissed.

With complex topics, it's harder to feel safe enough to say how we feel. But when the necessary tools are available, the group can start down the road to healing and reconciliation. I know that healing as a community will require many uncomfortable conversations.

What causes this discomfort? Our beliefs are not always rooted in logic. Sometimes, they are rooted in deep emotional pain. We need safe places where we can explore, question, critique, listen, and be heard, where everyone has a willingness to learn and not a desire to accuse. Let this verse guide our approach to discussions.

My dear brothers and sisters, take note of this: Everyone should be quick to listen, slow to speak and slow to become angry.
James 1:19, NIV

It's easy to get lost in the theoretical, so let's use a practical tool to evaluate how we behave when it comes to having critical conversations. Let's figure out how to create a space where hearts and minds are changed through expanded understanding. We must learn how to create safety before we speak the truth. We can deal more effectively with the content of an important conversation when we've acknowledged and processed the related emotions, which takes time and patience. It might even require a new level of strength and maturity.

Introduction

What does it mean to listen without agenda?

The purpose: To listen at the heart level to people, despite not being in full agreement with their views. We prioritize being aware of another person's verbal and nonverbal communication.

Try to understand other people. Forgive each other. If you have something against someone, forgive him. That is the way the Lord forgave you. Colossians 3:13, NLV

Speaking

How did the family you grew up in speak to one another?

In emotionally healthy communities, our comments are:

1. Respectful
2. Honest
3. Clear
4. Timely

Ask yourself this: In the last few days, when has *your* speech not been respectful, honest, clear, or timely? Imagine how you might have handled that interaction differently.

Listening

In emotionally *unhealthy* communities, people are expected to feel, think, and act the same way we do. When that doesn't happen, those who disagree might experience humiliation, isolation, judgment, and alienation.

In emotionally *healthy* communities, we give others the freedom and right to choose their own values, thoughts, and concerns.

As a deeply solution-oriented person, I have not always used this skill to connect with other people. My listening was really a form of interpreting. But then someone told me they didn't want to be "interpreted." They wanted to be understood—to be truly seen. Ironically, all my life, being misunderstood has been a source of pain and even fear for me—yet I was failing to truly understand others.

It can be hard to be emotionally open when you've been emotionally closed all your life. If you've endured extreme forms of mental stress, you might have grown up feeling lonely and misunderstood. Many people have never been listened to, by anyone. See Part 2 on the creation of Safe Spaces.

Questions to ask yourself when listening:

1. Are you considerate of the other person's position?
2. Do you listen to reply or to understand?
3. Are you listening with your needs in mind, or with the speaker's well-being in mind?
4. Is the conversation a dialogue (two-way) or monologue (one-sided)?
5. Do you give the speaker more room to speak? Do you ask for room to speak when you don't feel heard?

Workbook Activities

Partner Activity

1. Pair up with one person. Spread out as much as possible in the room.
2. Face each other and decide who will go first. Remember: This is designed to be a "win-win" exercise. As the speaker shares honestly and respectfully, your objective is to listen to your partner with sensitivity, respect, and empathy.
3. Each person will respond to the following questions: What is the biggest thing affecting you right now? How are you feeling about it?

As the speaker, remember to:

- Use "I" sentences. Sample answers: "I miss your company Jon, and I feel neglected" instead of "Jon, you are never emotionally available." "I got nervous when you did not show up on time." instead of "You are insensitive for not calling when you knew you'd be late."
- Keep your statements concise.
- Stop to let the listener summarize, because communication is also about what's being heard. It's not only about what's being said.
- Include your feelings. (For a list of feeling words, see the end of Chapter 8)
- Be clear, honest, and respectful.
- Be careful to distinguish a thought from a feeling.

As the listener, remember to:

- Give the speaker your undivided attention.
- Place yourself into the speaker's shoes and feel what they are feeling.
- Avoid making judgments or coming up with interpretations.
- Reflect back as precisely as you can what you heard them say.
- When you think the speaker is finished, ask, "Is there more?"
- When the speaker is finished, ask, "Of everything you have shared, what is the most important thing you want me to remember?"

In our culture, we often say, "I feel that…" to share a thought or opinion. A key principle to remember is when the word *that* follows "I feel" is an opinion or a thought, the speaker isn't revealing a real feeling. To use the phrase "I feel" correctly, it needs to be followed by a *feeling* (e.g., "I feel … sad, disappointed, anxious, happy," etc. We cannot get beneath the iceberg without sharing our feelings.

Examples:
An **opinion** statement: "I feel that these property taxes are too high." What you are really saying is: "I think (or I believe) that the property taxes are too high."
A **feelings** statement: "When I see my property tax bill, I feel worried and sad, because I'm not sure I can afford to live here."

4. Switch your roles as speaker and listener, answering the same questions.

   Note: As you share, consider the following areas: eye contact, facial expressions, body posture, head movement, wordless sounds (*ooo, ahh, oh*, etc.), tone of voice, and word choice.

Reflection Questions

1. What was the experience like for you as the speaker? As the listener?
2. How good was your family of origin at listening? Speaking?
3. Name one or two obstacles you will need to overcome to grow into a person who listens well.
4. Share your experience with one another by using the following sentence stems (one to two minutes each):
   a. "The most helpful thing the (listener/speaker) did was…"
   b. "What I would have liked more from the (listener/speaker) was…"

NOTES

These guidelines to listen without agenda are meant to be like the training wheels of a bicycle. The structure is necessary, especially in the beginning, to break deeply embedded bad habits.

This is tool is vital for emotional maturation—especially when the other person is saying something difficult to hear.

This is not a problem-solving skill. That will come in the section on Clean Fighting.

– 5 –

Assertiveness: Speak Your Peace From the Inside Out

Staying passively silent in the face of oppression slowly corrodes the soul.

The moment you think you can please everybody is the moment you guarantee yourself a life of burnout and constant frustration. Trying to live up to everyone's expectations is exhausting. If you do live up to everyone's expectations, you have more than likely crafted a false self. The false self is the gradual gathering of all the internalized messages and voices from people who want you to conform to their ideas of how you should be and what you should do. When you develop a false self, it causes you to lose touch with your true self.

The false self is the personality you construct that lives in response to what the outside world says instead of what you are naturally drawn to. Being who you are is probably one of the hardest things you'll ever have to do in life, because there will always be some conflict between your internal knowledge and social expectations. Far too many people live with their souls locked into someone else's tyrannical hold on their desires and wishes.

When we don't fit in, we either withdraw from social settings or are forced to see the world from many different points of view. I am a firm believer that each person is unique with their own individual way of thinking, feeling, and seeing the world. If you minimize your uniqueness to fit in, you waste your potential and unique contribution to the world. No two lives are the same, but often it seems that many lives look the same because people give in to the social pressure to conform. People generally have the tendency to follow the pack and might want to emulate other people. The pack has suggestions about what we should think or feel, and how we should behave.

We often fail to realize that every time we submit our uniqueness to someone else's opinion—of what we should like or who we should be—a part of us dies. It takes courage to truly be yourself and think your own thoughts.

You need tremendous discipline to be your true self. The true self represents values and desires that come from your own unique temperament, personality, and perspective.

Exercise

This self-assessment exercise will help you get a sense of where you are on the journey to being your authentic self. We all project different versions of ourselves sometimes, based on the environment we're in; but some people put on a mask of inauthenticity and settle for being fake. A mask helps hide a persona. We might wear a mask because we just don't know who we are or we're afraid to rock the boat by exposing who we truly are.

Have you been putting on a mask so that the people accept you? Let's take an assessment to determine if there is a part of you that has a false self. Take your time when reviewing this questionnaire. Don't feel rushed to complete this process. Give yourself the space to be reflective.

False Self-Assessment[i]

1. I often need approval from others to feel good about myself.
2. I often remain silent in order to avoid conflict.
3. When I make mistakes, I feel like a failure.
4. At times, I compromise my own values and principles to avoid looking weak or foolish.
5. My self-image soars with compliments and is crushed by criticism.
6. I do for others, at times, what they can and should do for themselves.
7. I am fearful and reluctant to take risks. My fears often cause me to play it safe, "just in case."
8. I often go along with what others want rather than "rock the boat."
9. I frequently compare myself to others.
10. My body is more often in a state of tension and stress than relaxed.
11. I have difficulty speaking up when I disagree or prefer something different.

How many of these statements resonated as true for you?

The point of this assessment is to make you aware of ways that you might not have been keeping it real with yourself and with others. This journey isn't about becoming something—it's about *unbecoming* everything that isn't you, so you can be who you were meant to be in the first place.

Becoming aware can sometimes be enough to make you want to change—but not always. If you've identified things that you are guilty of on this list, decide to do something about it. This does not mean that you should break out in rants about how you don't want to be controlled by anyone or make major, life-altering decisions impulsively. The assessment is meant to be a healthy self-reflection tool that will help you transition into the person you truly are.

When I was growing up, I learned quickly that the kid in the playground who doesn't want to fight always leaves with a black eye. I witnessed a startling level of violence and aggression in my neighborhood. I had to learn fast to stand up for myself, or life on the playground would be a series of challenges by the neighborhood bullies.

Bullies intimidate, coerce, manipulate, or harm weaker people with no consideration for their well-being. Their motivation is ignorance or selfishness. If you've been around long enough, I'm sure you've known a bully or two. They can be people in your community, your boss, friends, co-workers, and even parents. You might even have been a bully, intentionally or unintentionally.

I had to be prepared, at any moment, to protect myself and those I cared for. This was difficult for me since I was naturally a friendly kid who valued relational harmony. Sadly, my value system and the Newark playgrounds did not mesh too well. I chose to become **tougher (resilient, sturdy, durable), not meaner (malicious, pettily selfish)**. That's what differentiates those who create safety from those who create more chaos. **Get tougher, not meaner.**

In a safe space, we want to do quite the opposite of bullying. Instead of living in defense from bullies on the playground, we have an opportunity to create environments that encourage people to clarify their values by processing thoughts and feelings, and if necessary, by asserting themselves respectfully.

Many people confuse peace with quiet conflict. Quiet conflict is insidiously stressful. It affects us over time. This tool will allow people to *express their thoughts, feelings, values, and hopes* in a non-offensive way. This is speaking your peace from the inside out.

5: Assertiveness: Speak Your Peace from the Inside Out

This tool is used to address small, unclear, confusing, internal aggravations or irritations at their early stages. These things can be hard to articulate because they are small—but it's not always the big things that gets us in trouble. It's the little things. Many people manipulate situations instead of facing their own internal issues. This tool allows us to address these issues sooner rather than later.

The purpose of the tool: To clarify your values by your feelings and thoughts (and, if appropriate, to assert yourself respectfully).[5]

The Ladder of Integrity[6]

- Helps you get truthful and clear about what is going on inside of you.
- Helps you reveal and clarify your values so that you can assert yourself with the other person, if that is appropriate.
- Helps with addressing issues that might involve moral issues of right and wrong. Other issues might involve gray areas and personal preferences.

Important to Remember: This tool is not to be used for conflict resolution. It is about getting clear within yourself so you can identify your values, and then, if appropriate, respectfully share them.

Which of these values are most important to you?

Accomplishment o Achievement o Accountability o Accuracy o Adventure o Positive Attitude o Beauty o Calm o Challenge o Change o Collaboration o Commitment o Communication o Community o Comfort o Compassion o Competence o Competition o Connection o Cooperation o Coordination o Creativity o Decisiveness o Delight of being, joy o Democracy o Discipline o Discovery o Diversity o Effectiveness o Efficiency o Empowerment o Excellence o Fairness o Faith o Faithfulness o Family o Flair o Flexibility o Focus o Freedom o Friendship o Fun o Global view o Good health o Gratitude o Greatness o Growth o Happiness o Hard work o Harmony o Honesty o Improvement o Independence o Individuality o Inner peace o Innovation o Integrity o Intuitiveness o Justice o Knowledge o Leadership o Learning o Love o Loyalty o Management Maximum utilization (of time, resources) o Meaning o Modeling o Money o Openness o Orderliness o Passion o Peace – inner o Perfection o Personal Choice o Pleasure o Power o Practicality o Preservation o Privacy o Progress o Prosperity o Punctuality o Purpose o Recognition o Regularity o Relationships o Reliability o Resourcefulness o Respect for others o Responsibility o Results-oriented o Safety o Satisfaction o Security o Self-giving o Self-reliance o Self-thinking Service (to others, society) o Simplicity o Skill o Solving Problems o Speed o Spontaneity o Standardization o Status o Structure o Succeed; A will to o Success o Achievement o Teamwork o Techniques o Timeliness o Tolerance o Tradition o Transformation o Tranquility o Trust o Truth o Unity o Variety o Wealth o Wisdom

To use the ladder, we begin with Step #1 and work through the steps, being as honest as possible.

Model Climbing the Ladder of Integrity[7]

12 – I hope and look forward to....
11 – I think my honest sharing will benefit our relationship by....

What I Hope (11-12)

10 – The most important thing I want you to know is...
9 – One thing I could do to improve the situation is....
8 – I am willing or not willing to....
7 – This issue is important to me because I value....... and I violate that value when...

What I Value (7-10)

6 – What my reaction tells me about me is....
5 – My feelings about this are....

4 – My need surrounding this issue is….
3 – My part in this is….
2 – I'm anxious and talking about this because….
1 – Right now, the issue on my mind is….

What is going on inside me (**1-6**)

Be sure to stick to only one issue.

Individual Activity

1. Identify a non-volatile issue that is disturbing you. (e.g. messiness, texting at dinner, your family's holiday plans, somebody's tardiness, cancelling/missing meetings at the last minute, cell phone use while driving, TV or computer usage, lack of honesty)

    Note: Before you start, make sure that your issue is not because of faulty assumptions or failure to clarify expectations. See Chapter 2.

    Examples of issues based on failure to get information or clarify expectations:

    You call someone and leave three voicemails, but they haven't called back. You are so annoyed and bothered that you want to do a ladder about it. Before you start filling out the ladder, check out your assumption to be sure the other person even received the voicemails. You might simply need to say, "I'm puzzled why you have not called me back." You might learn that they never heard those messages (because of a lost or broken phone, etc.)

    Your twenty-year-old son and his girlfriend plan a vacation the same weekend as your family reunion. Did they know you expected them to attend the reunion? It might be that you have an expectation of them that is not realistic and to which they have not agreed.

2. Write down the issue by completing the following sentence stem:

   Right now the issue in my mind is…..

   Use "I" sentences that are respectful and clear.

   Examples:
   Disrespectful: "You don't care about canceling meetings at the last minute."

Respectful: "Right now the issue on my mind is that the last three meetings have been canceled at the last minute with no explanation."

Remember: This skill is not for confronting someone. It is to help you get clear internally.

- Once all blame has been removed, you are ready to talk to the other person.
- Many times, we will use the ladder and then realize we don't need to discuss the issue with anyone. The internal clarity obtained from going through the ladder is enough.

Opportunities to use the ladder of integrity:

- Marriage (if there is goodwill between the spouses)
- Parenting
- Workplace with your boss and/or colleagues.

It may take several times up the ladder to "mine" the real value that is involved.

Personal Action Steps

- Before the next session, write about a disturbing issue using the ladder of integrity to clarify your thoughts.
- After clarifying your thoughts and values, decide if it is appropriate to share with the person with whom you have the tension.

– 6 –

Clean Fighting: Words Can Bring Death or Life

Death and life are in the power of the tongue, and those who love it *and* indulge it will eat its fruit *and* bear the consequences of their words.
Proverbs 18:21, AMP

All close and authentic relationships will, at some point, be tested. Conflicts arise because each person has different perspectives, values, and priorities.

Most people are poor at resolving conflict because they have a limited understanding of peacemaking and a lack of training in the area of conflict resolution. Some people interpret peace as ignoring problems and difficult issues. Some choose to become people-pleasers and pacifiers.

We might fail to understand that conflict is not a bad thing. Conflict gives us the opportunity to learn about each other's values, priorities, and concerns. Resolved conflict can further deepen the closeness of a relationship. I know I have grown closer to the people in my life when we have resolved conflicts.

Many people ignore or avoid the tension of conflict because they were never taught how to resolve the issues in relationships. Unfortunately, bad things grow naturally, while good things have to be planted. For most people, the lessons on how to deal with issues in a healthy way are learned too late or not at all. When you avoid conflict but fail to resolve an issue, you are a false peacemaker.

Examples:

David is upset about his spouse constantly coming home late after work. He says nothing. Why? He thinks he's keeping things stable by not saying anything. Instead, he responds in passive-aggressive ways, like giving her the silent treatment. He is a false peacemaker.

Lily dislikes when her coworkers at lunch gossip about another coworker. She is reluctant to speak up. *I don't want to come across as a moral judge by speaking up and disagreeing,* she thinks. She is a false peacemaker.

Michael goes to dinner with five other people. He is on a tight financial budget, so he orders only a salad. Meanwhile, the other nine order appetizers, burgers, wine, and desserts. When the bill comes, someone says, "Let's divide up the bill equally. It will take forever to figure it out." Everyone agrees. Michael is dying on the inside, but he won't say anything. He is a false peacemaker.

Michelle is engaged. She would like more time to consider her decision, but is fearful that her fiancé and his family will get upset. She goes through with the wedding. She is a false peacemaker.

Kevin loves his parents. They are both quite critical about how he raises his children. Each family gathering is full of tension and frustration as his parents give him parenting advice, but he says nothing. He's a false peacemaker.

Jennifer thinks her boyfriend is inconsistent and irresponsible, but she feels sorry for him. He has had so much hurt already in his life, she thinks. *How can I add to that?* So she refrains from telling him the truth about the way his behavior is harming their relationship. The relationship dies a slow death. She is a false peacemaker.

True peace never comes by ignoring issues and problems. We might underestimate how deeply our bad habits are ingrained, but they won't go away on their own. With wisdom, we need to bring the issues to the light.

The worst time to learn conflict resolution is in the middle of a conflict. I'd like to provide you with a set of tools that will help you learn how to fight "clean." A clean fight is the mature resolution of a conflict, in which both people involved take responsibility for the issues. A clean fight is a negotiation between two people to find a resolution that will help protect their relationship.

Reflection Questions

In a word or two, how was conflict typically handled in your house growing up? (Some example answers are: yelling, avoidance, passive-aggressive actions, violence, denying, etc.).

The purpose of the clean fighting skill is to resolve conflict maturely by eliminating "dirty fighting" tactics and by taking responsibility for a difficult issue.

Dirty Fighting Tactics[8]

True peace will never come by pretending that what is wrong is right.

Exercise: Before we can walk through the steps of a clean fight, we need to raise our awareness of what dirty fighting looks like. Let's list the dirty fighting tactics that we might have learned. Use the section below to answer the following questions:

- What dirty fighting tactics have you used?
- Where did you learn these tactics?

Examples of dirty fighting tactics include: Silent Treatment — Sarcasm — Using "Always" or "Never" — Lecturing — Complaining — Anger/Rage — Blaming/Verbally Attacking — Denying — Escaping — Indulging in Addictions — Condescending — Walking Away — Passive-Aggressive Behavior — Making Threatening Gestures — Placating — Lying — Name-Calling — Avoiding — Hitting/Violence — Criticizing — Shouting — Showing Contempt

Please be honest about this. By doing this work, you are trying to break patterns of unhealthy conflict resolution to set the stage for a new way of doing things.

Clean Fight Model[9]

A clean fight is going to look and sound weird. You'll need to walk through the mechanics of this kind of negotiation over and over before you can get the hang of it. It's like riding a bike or driving a car. Once you've done it enough times, it becomes second nature—but at first, it takes a lot of practice. Remember, this work is about changing the unhealthy and dysfunctional ways that you may have done things in past relationships, so prepare for it to be uncomfortable.

1. Speaker: State the problem. "I notice …"
2. State why it is important to you. "I value."
3. Fill in the following sentence: "When you … I feel …"
4. State your request clearly, respectfully, and specifically.
5. Listener: Consider the request. In a few sentences, share your perspective on it.
6. Listener: Are you willing to do all of it, some of it, or none of it?
7. Speaker: Agree to or amend the request as needed.

Here's a practical example of how the clean fight is done.

Speaker:

- "I notice that when you borrow my car, you tend to block the sidewalk and not pull the car all the way up.
- "I value an unobstructed sidewalk."
- "When you block the sidewalk with your car, I feel anxious. I worry that our neighbors will think we're inconsiderate.
- "I would like to ask that you pull your car to the very end of the driveway when you arrive home first. If you forget, I would then like to ask that you take responsibility for moving both cars in all the way."

Listener:

- "I had no idea it bothered you. For me, it is no big deal to move the car. I am more than willing to do it. I have one adjustment, though. I would like to ask that you remind me nicely if I forget to do park the car correctly within thirty minutes."

Speaker:

- "It's a deal."

Things to Remember

If the other person offers an alternative, you can renegotiate—but not more than three times. If a proposal requires more than three adjustments, take a break, give it some thought, and try again later. You might need to get someone more objective—like a coach, counselor, or a mature friend—involved in the negotiation. This skill works best with issues that are non-volatile. Here are a few examples:

- I notice you call after ten p.m.
- I notice you don't answer my e-mails for at least four days.
- I notice you borrow my car at least once a week and rarely fill the tank.
- I notice you leave dirty dishes in the sink for more than a day.
- I notice when we are out to dinner, you pick your cell phone up at least three times.

Final Words[10]

- Conflict is normal, important, and essential if relationships are to enter the next level of growth and maturity.
- If you find yourself stuck in a fight that is complex, speak to a mature mentor or professional counselor. See the appendix on *Choosing a Counselor*.

Part 2

Safe Spaces Are Free of Chronic Tension and Anxiety—*You're Safe To Be Vulnerable*

The story of human suffering includes concepts like transgenerational epigenetic inheritance, hypothalamic pituitary adrenal gland and childhood adversity, intergenerational transmission of trauma, etc. These are SAT words that can make these problems sound super-complicated, which they can certainly be.

But on a much simpler level, these concepts describe the ways that we've been wounded, often early in life. They help provide a frame of reference for how we can heal to become a healthier as individuals and as a community. Even more specific than love, the word that keeps coming to mind is *safety*.

Some people grow up in safe environments. Others grow up in environments focused on survival. When it comes to family, one of the most important questions that should be asked is: Did you feel *safe* in the families you were raised in?

Many people have no idea what life in a safe home would look like. Chances are, if you've never been trained in the practical ways of showing love, you never learned, and you might end up picking up your behavior from the environment you were raised in.

Safe spaces give us permission to slow down the pace. We are allowed to love and be loved so we can be healed, affirmed, and validated in our God-given identities.

As I'm writing this, many mental health professionals are overworked because increasing social stressors and relational challenges have led to innumerable emotional, psychological, and behavioral issues. Often, the stressors we experience in our early lives are dealt with late in life. Sometimes, the consequences are forced upon folks through incarceration, divorce, bankruptcy, or some other life-altering circumstance.

People are often living their adult lives on top of their childhood experiences. For many, their internal lives have become unavailable.

Here are some statistics for you to consider:

- One in five people are living with a mental illness.
- The leading cause of death for black men under age forty-four is homicide.
- One in three in children are growing up without a father.
- One in three black male children will go to jail or prison at some point in their life.
- One in three women—and one in six men—are sexually abused before age eighteen.

Even if you have been educated about these statistics, you might not be mindful that these issues can affect people in both predictable and not-so-predictable ways. From my work over a decade, I have learned that the average person is carrying secrets that can be emotionally taxing to hold onto. As a result of unaddressed emotional wounds and persistent feelings of insecurity and inadequacy, many feel betrayed, tyrannized by pain, and unable to trust. As adults, they find they have no place to truly rest.

It's hard to cultivate a vision for your life if the trauma of your past blocks your perspective. We all come into relationships with pain and unfinished business from the past. There's some assembly required. We all have some gaps and deficits.

Those gaps and deficits carry over into adulthood and affect nearly every dimension of life, including our relationships, economics, vocations, and our communities. Our deficits can cause career missteps, poor life and relationship choices, wasted time, and continued emotional and mental pain. All of these consequences could have been prevented if the necessary tools were available.

Many of us have learned our life lessons the hard way, or we never learned them at all and are living lost, confused, and disillusioned with life. If this is you, please have compassion for yourself. It is unloving and unkind to expect yourself to do something that you were never taught how to do.

Many of us have never been taught how to live. We've been taught how to survive, how to get along without causing any trouble, and how to protect ourselves. But we've never been taught how to live wholeheartedly and abundantly. Fortunately, there's hope. Healing is possible. It is never too late to heal, grow, and to reposition yourself.

In this section, we will "kill multiple birds" with one stone:

1. Learning about the power of forgiveness
2. Processing our losses and identifying our triggers
3. Dealing with our self-worth/self-esteem issues as we reflect positively back on others

– 7 –

Forgiveness: The Cornerstone of Reconciliation

In the early part of the 20th century, the Belgian colonizers of Rwanda introduced a system of racism whereby Rwandan citizens over the age of ten would carry ethnic identity cards showing which tribe they belonged to. The tribal assignments were determined by Belgian scientists who measured heads, noses, height, skin color, and body shape. The scientifically superior tribe was named *Tutsi*. They were the Rwandans whose features most resembled European features. Those who appeared more African were called the *Hutus*. By creating these two classes, the colonizers intentionally introduced psychological feeling of inferiority in the Hutus. Their strategy was to divide and conquer.

Despite Tutsis being the minority, they held the power in Rwanda. Over the course of the 20th century, constant tensions existed between Tutsis and Hutus leading to revolutions, massacres, and refugees.

On April 6, 1994, Rwandan President Habyarimana, an ethnic Hutu, was killed after his plane was shot down near Kigali Airport. That evening, a genocide of all the Tutsis began. In 100 days, approximately 1 million moderate Hutus and Tutsis were murdered with machetes and guns.

The RPF (Rwandan Patriotic Front) liberated the nation and began working toward restoring order, which would be no small feat. To make the scenario clearer, imagine returning home as a soldier and seeing that ten, twenty, or thirty members of your family have been murdered. What would you do? The RPF (Rwandan Patriotic Front) prohibited revenge killings. Day and night, it was communicated through the ranks that the rule of law had to stand.

In an interview, the leader of the RPF was asked about his thinking behind keeping order after the genocide. There was one moment that stood out to me. He said that, in order for reconciliation to happen, someone has to absorb the pain. It was at the point that I knew that forgiveness is not only morally right, emotionally healing, and spiritually sanctifying—it is also socially redemptive. As a nation, you can't move on until you let go. The same applies to individuals.

This example has had a profound, formative effect on me. I've had situations in my life where the strength of my belief and conviction about forgiveness was tested. Let me rephrase—the *weakness* of my belief and conviction about forgiveness was tested. There were offenses against me that I did not let go and the longer I waited, the more I felt like I could not let them go. I held onto my anger for so long that the bitterness hardened my heart. Bitterness affected my language, my attitude, my trust of people, my vision, and my relationships. It also affected the ability to use my talents and gifts freely. Unforgiveness turned me into the worst version of myself. In addition to forgiving others, I had to forgive myself.

I've done some really foolish things over the course of my life. Some of those mistakes may still have effects on other people's lives today. In order for me to move forward with spiritual and emotional freedom, I needed to come to terms with the mistakes I'd made; grieve the pain I'd caused myself and others; and then let it go. This was and is still a continuing process, but the process is necessary and worth it. It allows me to live as the better version of myself. Forgiveness is a discipline that needs to be constantly practiced.

The great news is that we all have a choice. No matter how long it has been since the offense, we can learn to let go. We must come to see that forgiveness is not for the offender's benefit; it is for the offended. Forgiveness frees us to move on and allows us to give up victimhood. When we are no longer held hostage by the offense, we can find emotional freedom. We are more alive when we unyoke ourselves from the burden of anger we've been carrying.

It's certainly not easy to do. As a matter of fact, the forgiveness and the grieving process often go hand-in-hand, because many offenses come with a great deal of pain and sadness that can last a while. You have to pray for the strength and courage to deal with it—not run from it as so many people do. See chapter 8 for tools on the grieving process. Going through the grieving process is important and might need to be repeated.

Unforgiveness is ultimately selfish, because it causes you to see your life through a lens of fear, anger, resentment, or even hatred. These emotions rob you and the people you are here to help of the best version of yourself. Everything you create is influenced by your emotional and spiritual state. What you see with your eyes, hear with your ears, and say with your mouth is colored by the condition of your heart.

In a way, forgiveness can be seen as cutting your losses by releasing a losing investment and re-investing in things that matter. The next time you are tempted to hold a grudge against someone, think of someone you might be hurting and what you will lose by holding on to the grudge.

Take some time to journal your thoughts at the end of this chapter about where forgiveness might be needed in your life. Sometimes writing helps you to better process what you're feeling.

What Forgiveness Is Not

In talking about what forgiveness is, we need to discuss what forgiveness is *not*, in order to clear up confusion that exists in the culture.

1. **Forgiveness is not reducing the impact of the wrongdoing.** "No one's perfect." "Worse things have happened." These statements, though well-meaning, fall short of actually being forgiveness. If minimizing the wrongdoing becomes your normal way to dealing with minor offenses, you might avoid dealing with major wrongdoings with these statements as well. Be mindful to choose your words appropriately and with the seriousness required. You can forgive someone without trivializing the pain they caused.
2. **Forgiveness is not allowing wrongdoing to continue.** This is called enabling. Enabling is supporting someone in their irresponsibility or immaturity. Unfortunately, this gets confused all the time. Enablers are usually sweet, kind people who want to help. But it is important to be able to be stern with people and insist they treat you appropriately. Forgiveness does not mean you have to let someone continue doing the wrong thing.
3. **Forgiveness is not giving up or failing to acknowledge your pain.** Sometimes an offense against you can have lasting consequences and lead to ongoing pain. You can still forgive, so that you can heal. Forgiveness doesn't mean you are through feeling the effects of what was done.
4. **Forgiveness is not restoring trust.** You can forgive someone and still decide to never trust them again. Trust should be given based on evidence, not desire. See Chapter 9 on *Make Sure the Pearls are Safe Here*.

5. **Forgiveness is not avoiding the acknowledgment of a wrongdoing.** "I just moved on." "I didn't let it affect me." Sometimes people live in a state of denial, particularly after something really harmful was done to them. Out of fear or reluctance to face the truth, they avoid the full acknowledgment of what happened. You can forgive and still fully acknowledge what happened.
6. **Forgiveness is not waiting for an apology.** Some people will never be mature enough to acknowledge they were at fault. Some people will die before they come to terms with their offense. Don't wait until someone seeks forgiveness before you let go of their offense. I know it's not the most comforting thing to hear, but forgiveness is not for them. It's for you. You can still forgive, even if they're not sorry at all.
7. **Forgiveness is not forgetting.** The saying "forgive and forget" might be one of the biggest myths in our culture. It's a saying that doesn't possess much wisdom. There are some offenses that cannot be forgotten and some that should not be forgotten as a point of wisdom. If someone tries to kill me, you better believe I will never forget. I may forgive them, but if we ever cross paths again, wisdom will tell me to beware. We do not need to erase history in order to free ourselves from the past.
8. **Forgiveness is not a one-time event.** Sometimes forgiveness needs to be regularly chosen. Forgiveness is still effective, even if you have to repeat it.
9. **Forgiveness is not neglecting justice.** Justice and forgiveness can coexist. We must remember that what is sowed will be reaped. Actions have consequences, and consequences keep people from repeating mistakes. You can let go of the desire for revenge and forgive someone, but still maintain healthy boundaries by enforcing consequences.
10. **Forgiveness is not reconciling with the offender.** Forgiveness takes one person. Reconciliation takes two people. I know people who have gone through divorces, bad business partnerships, fractured friendships, and family drama. These situations sometimes have ripple effects that, unfortunately, keep people from being close again. Sadly, that is the reality of our world. Sometimes, it's best for people to be apart, because the pain of the offense is still too great. You can forgive someone and still decide to never have contact with them again.

Steps to Forgiveness

1. **Recognition:** Identify who you might need to forgive and how their offense or perceived offense has affected you. This may take some time. Grab a journal or sit down with a trusted friend and don't feel the need to write it all down at one time. Forgiveness will be more complete when you acknowledge what your betrayer has done to you.
2. **Release:** So many of us carry feelings of unforgiveness for so long that we constantly feel it and it almost becomes normal. Give yourself permission to get release through grieving and working through the pain, whether big or small. See Chapter 9 for a list of emotions. The stages of grief are avoidance, rage, negotiation, melancholy, and acknowledgment. By acknowledging the difficult emotions and working through them, you will begin to develop the strength to let go. You can choose to give up the desire to see the other person suffer as you have. All feelings of revenge and retribution need to be purged as part of forgiveness.
3. **Remove:** Remove any people or things that look to reinforce feelings of unforgiveness during the process. Your environment is extremely important to the type of person you want to become.
4. **Remind:** Remind yourself why forgiveness is important. Choose to walk in forgiveness from this day forth.

Other Ideas on Forgiveness

Forgiveness works well when it's not needed often.

Forgiveness is love repaired.

Weak people can't forgive. It's only something strong people can do.

– 8 –

Grieving: Joy Comes In the Mourning

Then Jesus went with them to a place called Gethsemane, and He told His disciples, Sit down here while I go over yonder and pray. And taking with Him Peter and the two sons of Zebedee, He began to show grief and distress of mind and was deeply depressed. Then He said to them, My soul is very sad and deeply grieved, so that I am almost dying of sorrow. Stay here and keep awake and keep watch with Me.
Matthew 26:36-38, AMPC

I want to be mature. I want to be a good example for the people I mentor. I want to be prepared as I work to master my work as a program builder. I want to keep my composure under control. I want to go hard until the end. These are the skills of good leaders: toughness, resilience, resourcefulness, stress tolerance, and fortitude.

What about learning how to grieve well? Why is that not a leadership skill that we need to cultivate? Some perspectives are incorrect. Some are incomplete.

No one can escape the impact of loss. The loss of someone who passes away, the loss of a friend through betrayal, the loss of health through illness, the loss of a marriage through a divorce, the loss of routines and stability due to a job loss or moving to a new country, the loss of innocence through abuse, the loss of the dream family through miscarriage, or the loss of a dream of a career. However big or small, everyone will go through loss in life.

The question is, how do we deal with loss and its accompanying pain? The way to deal with loss is through grieving. Grieving is not limited to tears. The grieving process could be through artistic expression, journaling, or helping someone else who has experienced loss. Grieving is any way of getting the pain that's inside out to the surface. Jesus said, "Blessed are those who gets mourn (get the pain of what's inside out), for they will be comforted" (Matthew 5:4).

The cause of depression for many people is untreated trauma, unprocessed emotions, and unresolved grief. One of the worst forms of emotional pain is the inability to communicate one's suffering.

In 2008, my cousin—who was more like my little brother—died at the age of seventeen. About a year later, I was arrested for DUI (driving under the influence).

For whatever reason, I couldn't make the connection between the two events. As I reflect on that time in my life, I didn't know how to properly grieve the loss, so I was thrown out of equilibrium, mentally and emotionally. Due to my lack of awareness, I made foolish choices rooted in a painful confusion and inattention.

The fallout, though it could have been worse, was ugly. This was the first time in my life that I had a loss so deep that it would be part of the fabric of my future choices. I was just starting my career, and unfortunately, I experienced several other losses in the same season.

An obvious but major truth is that, in these moments, "No one can know your sadness" (Proverbs 14:10, NCV). It's safe to say that I was experiencing a deep depression. I hid my emotional baggage, which was pretty easy—unfortunately, visible injuries get the most respect. Deep, internal sadness often goes unrecognized.

I was taught as a child that sadness is weakness, and that men are not allowed to be weak. Sadly, many others have also experienced this attitude. It took a few years and a lot of experiences working with people for me to realize how many other people carry deep, unspoken, and unaddressed pain rooted in their losses.

I learned the hard way that emotional wounds and underdevelopment are not always obvious when you first meet people, but they cause those people to struggle. It's hard to pursue a great life when you are emotionally wounded and stuck.

A major, and often unaddressed, part of emotional development and emotional well-being is learning to grieve our losses. If you or someone you know suffers a serious loss, you can help encourage them to go through the grieving process.

Guide to Grieving

1. **Identify your losses.** A loss is defined as the often-unanticipated, unrecoverable removal of something or someone in your life. Some things are not problems to be solved. Some things are truths that have to be accepted. Unfortunately, the truth doesn't always come without pain. You will more than likely have opportunities to walk through difficult moments in the life of someone you care for. It will help if you first expand your world view of pain and tragedy. Grieving your own losses allows you to grow compassion for others. One thing I've learned is that time will *not* heal all wounds. There are some wounds you must face head on with full acceptance, or they will insidiously interrupt your life forever.

    Consider that one in three children grow up without a father; one in three women and one in six men were sexually abused before the age of eighteen; and one in five Americans are dealing with a mental illness. In addition, more than 10,000 people are released from prison every week; often, they do not have adequate skills or tools to rebuild their lives.

In ***Bridge the Gaps – Lessons on Self-Awareness, Self-Development, and Self-Care***, I addressed several common losses that people endure. You might even understand them from personal experience.

We have the chance to experience tremendous healing if we identify our wounds, become aware of our feelings, and get to the root. One of the most difficult parts is working through the shame and embarrassment of the wound, but it's the most rewarding and takes away from the condemnation and pain that we carry around. All people have the capacity and the right to take time to heal themselves. See the chapters below. Learn more about this in these chapters from ***Bridge the Gaps***:

1. Mental Illness – Chapter 37
2. Colorism – Chapter 38
3. Sexual Abuse – Chapter 39
4. Fatherlessness – Chapter 40
5. Mass Incarceration – Chapter 41

2. **Recognize the stage of grief you're in.**
   Grief is like an onion. As you slice an onion, you'll discover that there are many layers. Also, there is no expiration date to grief. Anything can trigger the reminder of a loss: a movie, a random comment someone makes, the weather, a certain place you visit, etc. Each time you go through a layer, there are cycles you go through and you may need to revisit the cycle over and over. Here is a loose framework that you can use on your journey to healing from your pain. In especially heavy grief, you may go through the five-stage cycle several times until you have fully accepted the reality of your losses. A helpful acronym is ARNMA. They are:

   1. **Avoidance**—In this stage, there is a total avoidance and a focus on a false reality.
   2. **Rage**—This stage is where one recognizes that their false reality is

indeed false and then the rage sets in. This starts the thoughts of blaming, unfairness, and/or self-pity.
3. **Negotiation**—In this stage, the one experiencing the loss has some hope that the loss can be avoided or minimized in its severity.
4. **Melancholy**—This is a state of deep sadness and sometimes little movement and hopelessness.
5. **Acknowledgment**—In this stage, one embraces the loss or the inevitability of the loss.

These stages do not always happen in the same order. The purpose of this cycle list is to normalize your experience as you go through your grief. It can be a source of comfort as you process your pain to know this is not uncommon. Many cultures say that we should get over losses quickly, because sadness is a sign of weakness. People are not encouraged or allowed to be depressed.

We need a new culture that says:

- It's okay to acknowledge our losses.
- Processing our losses is important for our emotional development.
- We should pay attention to our losses and grieve those losses so we can be become more mature and compassionate.

3. **Identify your common defenses against grief.** Many people overestimate how well they control their emotional pain. A lot of us have learned to live with it for so long, it takes an outside event to force us to deal with the pain. For me, the outside event was a DUI. In many ways, these events can be a gift that opens up a pathway to change.

Some of the common defenses we use against experiencing grief include:

- Blaming
- Becoming hostile
- Intellectualizing
- Denial
- Distracting

- Rationalizing
- Over-spiritualizing
- Minimizing
- Medicating

I recently watched an interview of a man who suffered tragedy in his life. Part of the conversation went like this:
Interviewer: "Did you take time to grieve?"
Guest: "Not really. I numb when it gets hard."
Interview: "Is that healthy?"
Guest: "No, but it's practical."

This was an honest response and it is the way many people have been conditioned to process grief. Sometimes, due to the circumstances and demands of life, we have to "put our pain in a drawer." We might not be intentionally running away from it, but we know dealing with it will take more out of us than we can give at that moment. It's not for me to tell you when or in what precise way to feel and process your grief. I simply want to emphasize how important it is to do so, to live more fully and freely.

4. **Take time to regularly process your emotions**. There is no such thing as an unexpressed emotion. Everything you feel will affect you in some way. We often find ways to compensate for the void in our souls, through emotional triggers, overreaction, holding grudges, instant replay, insecurity, relationship issues, unhealthy patterns with inappropriate relationships, overspending (often on beauty and physical appearance—clothes, jewelry, etc.), over-exposure on social media, or illness, which allows us to attract attention. Why? Because if you don't deal with the pain, it will deal with you. Talking about our emotions is probably the easiest and most effective way to process them—but most people were not raised in environments where we could comfortably talk about emotions. We have a very limited emotional vocabulary and library. See the list of emotions in the next chapter – *Shame and Judgment: Do You Want to Get Well Again?*

5. **Talk to a therapist**. There are places inside us where we can't go by ourselves. Working through some of the previous tools alone will be a start, but it might not be enough to process all the losses you've experienced. We can't heal what we don't reveal. Sometimes, we think we're over things that have happened in our lives, but we're still showing symptoms that impact us in ways we don't even realize. Unresolved issues in your life will inevitably be exposed and will affect different aspects of your life. They often come from secrets. Holding on to secrets becomes a form of trauma. Revealing your secrets—or allowing someone to reveal their secrets to you—is often the first step in healing.

When I went to therapy and started to work through my emotional life, I came to realize I was sitting on a mountain of pain. As I spoke with a therapist, deeper levels of truth would emerge, and I was able to find a new sense of emotional freedom. It's not easy to do, but it's worth it. You might encounter a stigma in the black community concerning therapy. The only way to break the stigma is to tell our stories of life before and after therapy. Therapy will help you develop a recovery style that fits you, your temperament, and your situation as you pursue your own journey of healing.

– 9 –

SHAME AND JUDGMENT: DO YOU WANT TO GET WELL AGAIN?

Love requires that people know they are not alone.

Shame is a psychologically and emotionally crippling social issue. Shame is defined as a feeling of being broken, shoddy, and unfit for connecting with or being loved by others.

Shame says, "If you knew the truth about me, you would no longer love me." Sadly, the feeling of shame has become a public health issue, as it is correlated with mental health problems like depression, anxiety disorders, and addictions.

Shame arises out of false beliefs about ourselves and the world around us. It requires that we buy into the belief that we are alone.

The Man at the Pool of Bethesda

There was a certain man there who had been ill for thirty-eight years. 6 When Jesus noticed him lying there [helpless], knowing that he had been in that condition a long time, He said to him, "Do you want to get well?" 7 The invalid answered, "Sir, I have no one to put me in the pool when the water is stirred up, and while I am coming [to get into it myself], someone else steps down ahead of me."
John 5:5-7, AMP

When Jesus inquired about the man's desire to be well, the first thing the man replied with was an excuse, an attempt to avoid taking responsibility for doing his part to heal and be well again. The man, who had been ill for thirty-eight years, was suffering from learned helplessness. Learned helplessness simply means adapting the misery around you because you believe your performance will have no effect on the outcome. This means you believe your condition will be **permanent** (last forever), **pervasive** (affect all areas of life), and **personally** induced (all your fault).

If we are going to overcome shame, we have to fight against learned helplessness with everything we have. When we get to the root of the beliefs behind our shame, we can start to question them, using our logic and reasoning powers. Once we start questioning beliefs, we might realize that we don't actually agree with them, and from there, we can deconstruct them.

We don't have to be held hostage to the failures of yesterday, the sins we've committed, or the sins committed against us. Our struggles can keep us stuck in a cycle of self-doubt, shame, and guilt. Yet all of us have experienced career missteps, poor life and relationship choices, wasted time, and/or emotional and mental pain.

But as we noted before, many of us grew up without a good template to serve as our role model. When we encounter loss or even disappointment, we don't know how we should react, because we never saw an adult handle these things well.

If you grew up in survival mode, don't blame yourself for the skills you haven't learned yet. Your way of handling the normal disappointments of life might be based on self-protection. Your whole view of life might still be in "survival mode" if that was the way the adults in your early life existed. Forgive yourself for feeling lost or disillusioned, because your problems began long before you had any control over your life.

We all have, at one point or another, experienced shame. The good news is, once we have an idea of why we may feel the way we feel, we can take the steps to heal and grow into the people we were meant to be.

Shame needs *safety* to be undone. This is not an easy task. We can't heal problems that originate from shame without a perspective, a process, and a paradigm. Here are three tools to begin to cultivate safe spaces to heal shame, so that you can experience authentic living.

Three Useful Tools

1. *Cultivate Your Goodness*
2. *Drop Your Judgment*
3. *Acknowledge Your Wounds*

Make Sure the Pearls are Safe Here – Cultivate Goodness From the Inside Out

> *Do not give to dogs anything that is holy. And do not cast your pearls before swine, lest they trample them under their feet and then proceed to tear you to pieces.*
> Matthew 7:6, NCB

This verse, in its original context, advised that we should not allow the preciousness of spiritual truth to be ridiculed or to be vulnerable to those who would mock it. Culturally, this verse has been interpreted as meaning we should not share what is important and sensitive to those who would not handle it with care as you would a delicate, precious object.

What immediately comes to mind are people's secrets. Statistics we shared in the beginning of this section show that many of us carry secrets. This is true in communities across this country.

By cultivating goodness from the inside out, we can help address these secrets. We can create safe spaces for people and work to address the systems to perpetuate the ongoing pain that people suffer.

Goodness is righteousness in action. Righteousness is about setting things *right*, as they should be. It leads to actions and works that serve others. It comes from having a heart that wants to help others and make the world a better place. It's start inside and then works itself out.

Cultivate Goodness on the Inside

Some years ago, I attended a special church service called the "Right Hand of Fellowship." This was back when all the new members of the community were formally presented, prayed for, and welcomed into the church. The pastor stood at the podium and explained what it means to be part of a community. In his own words:

> *"We appreciate the value of community and family and want our community and family to be healthy and strong. We will ask you to leave if you do this one thing. Adultery never destroyed a church. Drug abuse never destroyed a*

church. Alcoholism never destroyed a church. But gossip has. If you gossip, we will ask you to leave. Nothing has destroyed a community faster than gossip, because people no longer feel safe to be honest about their struggles."

When I heard these words, it felt like everything stopped. I had to reevaluate my life and how I might have played a role in hurting my community and my family. His words rang so true, I decided that day that I would become a secret-keeper—someone who could be trusted to hold on to the secrets of others.

The Scripture says that a gossip betrays a confidence, so we should avoid anyone who talks too much (Proverbs 20:19, NIV). A true friend is a vault; they don't share your secrets with anyone, and they don't share with you anything that's not theirs to share.

I adopted a no-gossip policy in my life some years ago. Gossip means bearing bad news behind someone's back with impure motives.

This decision was a life-changing for me. It helped me understand why trust breaks down in communities.

As a result of being acutely aware of the practice, I recognized that most people don't realize how unsafe they are. There is nothing that makes me lose trust in someone faster than when they share with me the private details of other people's lives.

As someone who grew up deeply rooted in church, I had a fair share of good and bad experiences. I knew great people who were warm, approachable, agreeable, and humble. Unfortunately, I met others who did not exude these qualities.

What was confusing to me initially was that many of these people meant well but didn't do right. The toughest thing that I've ever had to reconcile was that I was raised in communities where I was confident that I was loved, but that practice of love wasn't reflected in a helpful way. Unfortunately, I know I'm not alone in that observation. Many people leave the church on steady basis because of the hurt they experience from the inconsistency and blatant hypocrisy of people who profess to follow Jesus. It's easy to profess to have beliefs in Jesus without those beliefs being "fully developed in your lives." (Galatians 4:19, NLT)

After some reflection, I came to the realization that communities are like a garden. Bad things grow naturally. Good things have to be planted. Much of the relational pain we experience can be avoided if we have the right tools to create safe spaces to prevent and heal relationship hurt and breakdown.

Safe communities don't allow people to be dehumanized, degraded, or demoralized in the name of culture. You can change the behavior, but if you don't change the culture, the behavior will come back. If you're ever had your trust broken, you probably know the feeling of "I will never trust anyone, ever again!"

Gossip is a betrayal, and it creates a certain level of anxiety, frustration, and abandonment in people. Safe spaces are needed to resolve emotional issues that take time to settle.

The average person is carrying secrets that can be emotionally taxing. We can lighten their load by adopting new practices, such as holding space for them to work things out. Sometimes people don't need to share the details, they just need the space to process.

How can you heal in the same kind of environment that made you sick? You need to change the dynamics of the environment. Things won't change without intervention. In order to make new decisions, you need new habits, new practices, and new disciplines. In addition to the skills learned in Part 1, we are mindful to create spaces that keep people safe from shame and judgment. Let this section take it a step further and identify practices to guard against that can create danger in communities.

Types of Unsafe People/Actions in a Community

The five kinds of people that create unsafe communities are: the mocker, the judgmental onlooker, the gossip, the instigator, and the busybody.

Mocker/Scoffer/Ignorant Fool

These are people who tease in a belittling and malicious way. They stifle progress by holding important things in contempt. They discuss important matters in a frivolous and foolish way.

Get rid of the one who makes fun of wisdom. Then fighting, quarrels, judgments, insults, and shame will stop.
Proverbs 22:10 EXB

Stay away from fools because they can't teach you anything.
Proverbs 14:7 EXB

Judgmental Onlookers/Hypocrite

They teach truth but have no grace, mercy, or compassion. They are like judges or referees instead of loving coaches or teachers.

The teachers of the law and the Pharisees......follow whatever they tell you, but their lives are not good examples for you to follow. They tell you to do things, but they themselves don't do. They make strict rules and try to force people to obey them, but they are unwilling to help those who struggle under the weight of their rules.
Matthew 23:1-4, EXB

You appear, at first blush, to be righteous, selfless, and pure; but on the inside you are polluted, sunk in hypocrisy and confusion and lawlessness.
Matthew 23:28, VOICE

The Good Samaritan Story: *Jesus said, "A man was going down the road from Jerusalem to Jericho. Some robbers surrounded him, tore off his clothes, and beat him. Then they left him lying there on the ground almost dead. 31 It happened that a Jewish priest was going down that road. When he saw the man, he did not stop to help him. He walked away. 32 Next, a Levite came near. He saw the hurt man, but he went around him. He would not stop to help him either. He just walked away. "*
Luke 10:30-32, ERV

Gossipers

They reveal information that was unknown or unseen by others, and they do it recklessly or with bad intent. They have no discretion or no concern for how gossip can hurt the hearer and the gossip victim. Gossip is spiritual poison. In a way, it's like trying to be God—speaking a word for your agenda.

Gossips can't keep secrets, so avoid people who talk too much.
Proverbs 20:19 EXB

If you don't have wood, your fire goes out. If you don't talk about others, arguing dies down.

When there is no wood, the fire goes out. Where there is no one telling secret stories about people, arguing stops.

Proverbs 26:20, NIRV, NLV

Dishonest people use gossip to destroy their neighbors; good people are protected by their own good sense.

Proverbs 11:19, CEV

Instigator/Troublemaker

A troublemaker defies those in authority with reckless or destructive motives and causes constant problems in a community. They disrupt harmony and trust. They inflame the emotions of others to do wrong.

A troublemaker plants seeds of strife; gossip separates the best of friends.

Proverbs 16:28, NLT

The words of a whisperer or slanderer are like dainty morsels or words of sport [to some, but to others are like deadly wounds]; and they go down into the innermost parts of the body [or of the victim's nature].

Proverbs 26:22, AMPC

The words of a whisperer (gossip) are like dainty morsels [to be greedily eaten]; They go down into the innermost chambers of the body [to be remembered and mused upon].

Proverbs 18:8, AMP

Stay away from people who talk about useless things that are not from God. That kind of talk will lead a person more and more against God. Their evil teaching will spread like a sickness inside the body. Hymenaeus and Philetus are men like that.

2 Timothy 2:16-17, ERV

Busybody

The two best descriptions of a busybody are "spy" and "intruder." Busybodies ask intrusive and inappropriate questions, especially of those with whom they don't have a trustworthy rapport. They regularly offer unsolicited advice, which even if they are well-meaning, is motivated by their own sense of discomfort with uncertainty. At worst, getting information like this is a form of manipulation to control someone's life. Their show of support is often a kind of surveillance. The line of questioning and subsequent actions will indicate whether there is true concern for one's well-being or just a desire to learn of one's affairs. Some people don't care about your well-being. They just want to understand you so they can talk about you.

You may suffer, but don't let it be because you murder, steal, make trouble, or try to control other people's lives.
1 Peter 4:15, ERV

Like one who grabs a dog by the ears [and is likely to be bitten] is he who, passing by, stops to meddle with a dispute that is none of his business.
Proverbs 26:17, AMP

Reflection Questions

No one is perfect. In the spirit of walking in the light and taking the log out of your own eye, take time to review these actions. Could you be described as one of the above types? Have you become accustomed to tolerating this kind of unsafe behavior in others?

CASUAL Community

The word casual means *relaxed and unconcerned*. In a casual community, you are relaxed because you feel safe.

Leadership for safe community consists in cultivating, carrying, and protecting safe space in which people's full humanity can be seen. By no means can you trust everyone with information about your personal struggle, nor should you. However, you should stive to create a community where you and others feel it is safe to be authentic.

People lie when they don't feel it is safe to tell the truth. A safe community is important because it creates a conducive environment for people to speak deeper levels of truth. People can emotionally "disrobe" and become vulnerable. That requires that safety is used consistently.

Healing cannot happen without the truth. Some people have challenges that merit specific, skilled help—but many mental and emotional struggles can be healed in the context of a safe community.

Shame and lies keep us locked up. Compassion and empathy can set us free.

You need to cultivate good "people radar" because, like the Pharisees, people can "*appear good to everybody, but inside are… full of hypocrisy and sins.* (Matthew 23:28, GNT)

Here are some things people can do in a safe, casual community:

- **Clear up assumptions and clarify expectations** – Have the courage to have a conversation with a friend instead of making up a story about a situation. Be generous in interpretation and assumption of the situation and turn to wonder.
- **Admit their wrongs and accept your individuality** – They own their mistakes and respect your choices even if they don't agree.
- **Be a secret-keeper** – They protect your confidences and also refuse to share the confidences of others.
- **Be undivided and word-honoring** – They remain a person of integrity and keep their promises.
- **Avoid judgment** – They put themselves in your position and don't make themselves feel superior to you.
- **Respect limits** – They know how to treat you and know what's okay and what's not okay in a relationship with you.

Just as a reminder, the skills in Part 1 are ones that we want to regularly practice in a community where we can speak clearly, respectfully, and honestly. Like any skill, we must intentionally practice these skills on a consistent basis by:

1. Expressing appreciations and sharing new information (Ch.1)
2. Clearing up assumptions and setting valid expectations (Ch.2)

3. Understanding your family background and what cycles need to be broken (Ch.3)
4. Listening without an agenda (Ch.4)
5. Speaking your values in a safe space (Ch.5)
6. Fighting cleanly (Ch.6)

Cultivate Goodness on the Outside

One Sabbath, when Jesus went to eat in the house of a prominent Pharisee, he was being carefully watched. There in front of him was a man suffering from abnormal swelling of his body. Jesus asked the Pharisees and experts in the law, "Is it lawful to heal on the Sabbath or not?" But they remained silent. So taking hold of the man, he healed him and sent him on his way. Then he asked them, "If one of you has a child or an ox that falls into a well on the Sabbath day, will you not immediately pull it out?" And they had nothing to say.
Luke 14:1-6, NIV

In this story, Jesus asks the Pharisees which is more important: the rule of law, or the *spirit* of the rule of law. The basic dignity and genuine needs of human beings are more important than following rituals and practices for their own sake. When a rule undermines its intention, it should be reconsidered, or the act should be an accepted deviation, because the greater principle was upheld. The worst thing we can do is follow a rule just because it's in place, when there are more effective and honorable alternatives.

Geoffrey Canada understands this all too well. He is the black anti-poverty reform advocate and founder of the Harlem Children's Zone, a pioneering non-profit organization committed to ending generational poverty. His organization has served more than 10,000 children over the last twenty years.

Based on Canada's experience in the 1950s and 1960s, in order for the black people in his mother's generation to get a job, they had to be subservient to their white bosses. Racial dehumanization was so ubiquitous in workplaces that black people were forced to bow down and compromise their dignity to put food on the table. They had to "know their place." They couldn't speak up, or they would be fired.

Because of white dominance and subjugation, many black people were forced to bow down symbolically. They realized how hard the fight against racism would be and acknowledged that life was already hard and short, so they acquiesced to the unfair, racist society.

Unfortunately, many black parents passed these survival practices down to their children. Their children also inherited the accompanying perceptions, interpretations, opinions, assumptions, and beliefs about the world—and in many ways, the mindset disempowered them.

I am thankful for those who came before me who made it possible to exercise a greater level of courage in the fight for justice and progress of black people in America. Slavery survival practices might have been appropriate in adapting to a hostile environment, but they could not be a final solution for people living in a just society.

Acquiescing to injustice also is contradictory to brain science. A person's mind needs to be stimulated to progress and develop in a healthy way. The brain requires active exploration, feedback, challenge, and creative work to get the most out of an educational experience. Essentially, many black parents were teaching their children to be afraid, mediocre, and subservient.

Most parents give their children advice based on their experience. If the dynamics of their experience is anything similar to the type mentioned above, the advice will often be disempowering. If an oppressive, racist system signs your paychecks, passes laws, creates policy, and interprets the world, that system influences your culture.

When those in power are indifferent to the way they harm those subordinate to their authority, they force their subordinates to capitulate to the system, fall into despair and possibly pathology, or rebel and revolt by any available means. This has been my observation.

Refusal to play by the wrong rules means breaking the rules. Something may be a prevailing practice, but that doesn't mean it's moral, useful, or necessary. We have been trained by explicit and unwritten rules on how we should live, what we can achieve, and ultimately, who we might become. But what happens when rules (explicit and societal) don't serve the best and highest purpose? What happens when social/cultural rules and standard professional practices keep you from doing your best and most honorable work?

Then you must break the rules. But how?

I completely recognize that this question is worthy of significant time to unpack. The unique dynamics in the black community have not been slow in the making, and they will not be quick to unravel. As a result, we need a depth of knowledge, critical thinking, and a level of emotional maturity.

A Rule that I live by: Read the books and make up your own mind.

1. *The Bridge to Change: Mentoring Tools for Parents, Teachers, Coaches and Counselors* by Jonathan Frejuste
2. *Dare to Lead: Brave Work. Tough Conversations. Whole Hearts.* By Brene Brown
3. *Intelligent Disobedience: Doing Right When What You're Told to Do Is Wrong* by Ira Chaleff
4. *The Courageous Follower: Standing Up to and for Our Leaders* by Ira Chaleff
5. *I Write What I Like: Selected Writings* by Steve Biko
6. *Strength to Love* by Martin Luther King, Jr.

2 – Drop Your Rocks and Look in the Mirror: Create Culture of Unconditional Love and Character Development

> *Don't pick on people, jump on their failures, criticize their faults—unless, of course, you want the same treatment. That critical spirit has a way of boomeranging. It's easy to see a smudge on your neighbor's face and be oblivious to the ugly sneer on your own. Do you have the nerve to say, 'Let me wash your face for you,' when your own face is distorted by contempt? It's this whole traveling road-show mentality all over again, playing a holier-than-thou part instead of just living your part. Wipe that ugly sneer off your own face, and you might be fit to offer a washcloth to your neighbor.*
> Matthew 7:1-5, MSG

It's been said the worst kind of army is one that shoots its own wounded. That "army" could be a family, an organization, or a house of worship. Let's take this opportunity to review the cultures created in each place and beyond.

The safest environments are ones that work diligently foster two things:

1) Grace – "unearned, undeserved favor and spiritual blessing," (John 1:17, AMPC)
   When Grace speaks:
   - Grace says you are safe from abandonment, condemnation, and disposability.
   - Grace says we were made to operate *from* approval, not *for* approval.

2) Truth – "absolutely free of deception." (John 1:14, AMP)
   When Truth speaks:
   - Truth says that there must be a commitment to reality at all costs.
   - Truth ensures that you put principles, boundaries, and expectations in place so you don't fall again. (See Chapter 15)

There is a story in the Good Book that explain the perspective of grace and truth, which I believe serve as the cornerstone of safe communities. Please read the story and answer the reflection questions.

The Woman Caught in Adultery

The teachers of the law and the Pharisees brought in a woman caught in adultery. They made her stand before the group and said to Jesus, "Teacher, this woman was caught in the act of adultery. In the Law Moses commanded us to stone such women. Now what do you say?" They were using this question as a trap, in order to have a basis for accusing him. But Jesus bent down and started to write on the ground with his finger. When they kept on questioning him, he straightened up and said to them, **"Let any one of you who is without sin be the first to throw a stone at her."** *Again he stooped down and wrote on the ground. At this, those who heard began to go away one at a time, the older ones first, until only Jesus was left, with the woman still standing there. Jesus straightened up and asked her, "Woman, where are they? Has no one condemned you?" "No one, sir," she said.* **"Then neither do I condemn you,"** *Jesus declared.* **"Go now and leave your life of sin."**

John 8:3-11, NIV

Reflection Questions

What are the themes in this story?
Why do you think the older ones left first?
How was safety created in this story?
Where is the grace illustrated in this story?
Where is truth illustrated in this story?

Over a decade ago, I was arrested for driving under the influence. At the time of the arrest, I was sitting on the board of trustees of my high school alma mater, the treasurer of a grassroots organization focused on community development, and a mentor to several young people. I had two choices: I could play the cover-up game, or I could come clean to everyone I was accountable to. The cover-up game is very tempting after you've done something stupid, but I believe the long-term effects would have been detrimental. The right thing to do is usually the hardest.

I chose to come clean and as a result, contrary to my belief at the time, I was praised for my honesty and integrity. We live in a world where people are always covering up or twisting the truth to not reveal their mistakes—so much so that, when someone is honest, it's surprising and refreshing. I believe that our culture needs to shift from loving to see people "get caught" to loving to see people "come clean," because the truth is that no one is perfect. And once we all stop faking it, maybe we can give each other the safe space we need to change.

Now, that doesn't mean that you should go on social media and tell the world about your deepest, darkest secrets or indiscretions, but it does mean that you need safe spaces where you can work through the issues in your life that are keeping you from being your best self with the utmost character and integrity.

After that experience, I began a season of counseling which lasted several years. In this season, I was loved unconditionally and my sense of self could be fortified in a safe and forgiving space. Without that season of my life, I would not have had the space to cultivate the courage and the clarity to write several books and launch a comprehensive life-coaching program that serves universities, prisons, churches, and substance abuse centers.

I came to the realization that good seed cannot grow in contaminated soil. Doing the work of healing your trauma gives you room to cultivate a vision for your future.

Two seemingly paradoxical things happened to me in therapy. I was given the space to be imperfect and also challenged to work on my character deficiencies. Practically, I was given the space to:

1) Create a shame-free culture
2) Develop an unassailable character

Create a Shame-Free Culture

A healthy family is achieved when we leave the nightlight on for those who have wandered away.

One of my greatest realizations is that your upbringing and/or family of origin is primarily where you learn how to be a victim or a survivor. You are supposed to learn who you are and have your authentic self-fortified as you grow up. Unfortunately, many people do not know this experience. In fact, most people are conditioned to disconnect from their authentic selves and to live out the lives of other people. In the process, they develop a shame-based identity.

To remind you of the definition of shame, it is a feeling of being broken, shoddy and unfit for connection with and love from others. Shame is the emotion that says, "If you knew the truth about me, you would no longer love me." Feelings of shame are so common, they are considered a public mental health issue that can lead to depression, anxiety disorders, and addictions.

Communities that produce shame generally have these unspoken rules or commandments:

- Never ask for help because people who ask for help are weak.
- Don't rock the boat as long as our image looks good. It's about perception, not reality. This encourages secrets and secrets make us sick.

- Don't trust anyone because they will exploit your weakness and hurt you. Reminder: We are to set standards for the people in our lives. See the previous section – *Make Sure the Pearls are Safe Here* – CASUAL Community
- Don't question your parents no matter what they do. You owe them your loyalty because they always know what's best.
- Find a "black sheep" to blame for all our problems because if we acknowledge our own mistakes, it will make us feel defective.

Some of us carry guilt from things we've done in our past. These are things we may have come to terms with and paid for, or things that were unseen by the world at large. We have to fight through the mistakes we've made. Failure does not disqualify you from being loved.

One of the ways you can know if you're in shame is if you hear tapes playing in your head that say, "You're not good enough" and/or "Who do you think you are?" Without disclosing the names of individuals, here are some specific internal messages that others have told me they hear repeatedly:

- You failed the CPA exam five times. You're not really smart. You just got lucky.
- Who are you to write a book? You didn't go to school for this.
- You had a baby out of wedlock. You can never have a better life.
- Your child is in prison. You must not be a good parent.
- You've been used and abused. No one will want you.
- Why are you going back to school now? Will you even be able to keep up?
  - All you did before was fail. What's going to change if you try again?
- You dropped out of school. You're not educated. No one cares about your opinion.
- Now that you're married, why can't you have a baby? What's wrong with you?
- You had an abortion. This mistake can never be erased. This will haunt you.
- You are not married yet. Something must be wrong with you.

- You can't have a child. You are defective and worthless.
- Why are you crying? Real men don't cry.
- Why are you still unemployed? You should've finished college.
- You're a felon/ex-con. No one will hire you.
- Why didn't you buy a house?
- When are you going to have children?

I know these are difficult messages to read, but they are real, and we can't heal unless we bring these things into the light and deal with them. Unfortunately, these kinds of messages are planted into our minds and hearts from our upbringing and our families, friends, and cultures. Some people spend their whole lives overcoming the negative messages from their past. These messages perpetuate a continuous sense of inadequacy instead of bringing about hope for redemption and encouragement to learn from our pain.

Shame is strengthened by three things:

1) **Secrets**—Shame is tough, but it is nothing in comparison to knowing that you are required to keep your mouth shut about something. We are as sick as the secrets we keep. Finding a safe place to help you unload your burdens can help you tremendously. A support group, a church meeting that focuses on your particular struggle, or a trusted and competent counselor/coach can help you heal. The prior chapter shares a powerful lesson on how to evaluate safe people to speak to. Also, the appendix will include pointers on choosing a counselor.

2) **Elephants in the room**—When tough issues like the scenarios mentioned above are not put on the table to be discussed, their power to disrupt your emotional and psychological state grows. It also destroys your ability to have true intimacy and community and sometimes leads to worse things, which include medicating your pain with substances like food, alcohol, or drugs, or overspending, acting out sexually, and being around unsafe and/or unhealthy environments.

3) **Judgment or condemnation**—Attacking others gives some people a false sense of superiority. It's easier to hurt others than to identify

with them. Because once you identify with someone, you place both parties on level ground, and some people always want to have a sense of superiority which many times is rooted in insecurity. Many people judge in the name of, "I'm just telling the truth." Word to the wise: Truth can be used as a sword or a scalpel: A scalpel is a medical device that helps to cut for the purpose of healing. A sword is used to bring harm. Be mindful of your intent and the effect of the truth as you relay a message to someone. Ask yourself these questions before you speak a truth:

a. Is it true?
b. Is it helpful?
c. Is it inspiring?
d. Is it necessary?
e. Is it kind?

I am learning every day the degree to which people were not affirmed, myself included. As a result, I am learning to develop the habit of being encouraging and speaking life, especially when providing constructive feedback. Causing unintentional shame is still painful. I want to help others overcome self-doubt and believe they are enough.

Shame can be removed by using:

1) **Compassion and empathy.** Empathy is important to recovery. Compassion is the ability to have concern for the suffering of other people. Empathy is putting yourself in someone else's shoes. Advice: The next time you see some type of abuse of a human being, take it personally. The way to truly create a safe and healthy community that fights shame is for everyone in that community to not tolerate it.

2) **An awareness of your shame triggers.** A trigger is something that sets you off emotionally. Everyone has a different set of triggers. Many times, your shame triggers come from your childhood or maybe some difficult or traumatic experience you had in the past. For me, it's in the area of academics. I didn't feel smart as a kid because of bad messaging from

well-intentioned but unwise people who called me derogatory names, thinking their insults would motivate me to do better in school. Words do hurt and they can affect the course of someone's life. The tongue has the power of life and death. (Proverbs 18:21, NIV)

I walked around feeling dumb and destined to fail in school and ultimately in life. It took a lot of prayer, work in counseling, and self-awareness to realize this was not the case. Now I have identified my triggers and work to stay confident in my abilities. I try to be honest about my weaknesses. I had to have compassion for myself and give myself room to be imperfect.

We all have areas where we feel shame. Much of the work involves figuring out your triggers and being prepared to fight against them so you can move through life without letting shame paralyze you. Common shame triggers include references to body image or physical appearance, abuse, financial status, intelligence (particularly when it comes to getting a degree or certification), parenting, past sexual relationships, and legal history. You might be able to add to this list. The point is that these issues may affect your life, but they should not and do not affect your self-worth. That's where the work needs be done. Get aware. Get honest. Get healed and walk in freedom. Easier said than done, I know, but you have to get started to get to emotional freedom. Find a place that's safe, like a counselor's office or a support group, and get to work dealing with your shame by affirming your intrinsic value: your value apart from any accomplishment, position, possession, appearance, title, or skill. Only then can you get perspective on what you are here to do. I pray for your courage in dealing with these issues and getting your life back from shame.

3) **Identifying shame messages**. These are part of the culture you're in, so you'll need to push back. We must learn when to take responsibility and also when to oppose the views of the culture that perpetuate shame. This awareness includes three things:
   a. Investigating why certain messages exists.
   b. Determining how these messages impact the community.
   c. Determining who gains from the messages.

Once we've done this work, we can boldly proclaim that we are not broken or defective. We are enough, and out of the sense of being enough, we can live more full, impactful, and wholehearted lives.

A word to anyone who works with people in any capacity:
Guilt and shame are two tools that are sometimes used in working with people. Guilt says you *did* something bad. Shame says you *are* bad. Guilt focuses on behavior. Shame focuses on the person. Shame is a dangerous tool to use to change behavior. It often causes more harm than good and perpetuates a negative culture that emotionally abuses in order to achieve progress. Results may be achieved in the short term, but over time, shame has damaging effects on a person's soul and ultimately their community. Guilt, however, affirms the dignity of the person while correcting mistakes or bad behavior. Remember to focus on guilt and not shame.

If you work with people, please remember this: "Be kind, because everyone is fighting a battle you know nothing about."

Wrap words around your shame story

Shame hates having words wrapped around it. We have the chance to experience tremendous healing if we identify our wounds, become aware of our feelings, and get to the root. One of the most difficult parts is working through the shame and embarrassment of the wound, but doing this work is the most rewarding and takes away from the condemnation and pain that we carry around.

I encourage you to review the list above and think about situations you've experienced. Our woundedness reflects itself in our choices, understanding, morals, and judgment. Most people I know have had painful, emotional, shame-filled moments in life that might have made their internal lives inaccessible.

When you decide to feel your own hurt, you grow compassion for yourself and others. You can become an example of how to courageously confront pain. Situations like the ones above perpetuate cycles of shame, doubt, and guilt. Here's a process to help you get in control of painful words and/or situations:

1. When a tough emotional experience or conversation happens, it is probably going to take some courage to get curious about your emotional state. Our emotions get the first word when we go through situations in life. Feelings are real, but that doesn't mean they are always the truth or that they have the final word in your destiny. There are a whole host of dysfunctional responses to these emotions, including blaming, overeating, looping thoughts, violence, excessive niceness, etc. Many of the responses are an attempt to numb yourself from the pain. People across the world have a numbing issue. The problem is that dysfunctional responses can show up in ugly ways: depression, anxiety, insomnia, etc. When something disturbing happens, take time to notice what's going on, physically and emotionally. Using the list of emotions at the end of this tool, what emotion are you feeling? What is happening in your body: stomach ache, stiff neck, back pain?

_____

_____

_____

List of Emotions
Joy – Tenderness – Defeat – Rage – Cheer – Sympathy – Powerlessness – Boredom – Outrage – Contentedness
Adoration Dread – Rejection – Hostility – Pride – Fondness – Distrust – Disillusionment – Bitterness – Satisfaction Receptivity – Suspicion – Inferiority Hate – Excitement – Interest – Caution – Confusion – Scorn – Amusement Disturbance – Grief – Spite – Shock – Overwhelm – Helplessness – Vengeance – Enthusiasm – Exhilaration – Discomfort – Isolation – Dislike – Optimism – Dismay – Guilt – Numbness – Resentment – Elation – Amazement Hurt – Regret – Trust – Delight – Confusion – Loneliness – Ambivalence – Alienation – Calm – Stun – Melancholy Exhaustion–Relaxation – Interest – Insecurity – Insult – Relief – Intrigue – Disgust – Indifference – Hope – Absorption – Sadness – Pity – Pleasure – Curiosity – Revulsion – Confidence – Anticipation – Hurt – Contempt

– Bravery – Eagerness – Weariness – Hesitancy – Safety – Fear – Depression – Preoccupation – Happiness – Anxiety Anger – Love – Worry – Sorrow – Jealousy – Lust – Terror – Uncertainty – Envy – Anguish – Annoyance – Disappointment – Humiliation – Compassion – Self-consciousness – Irritation – Caring – Alarm – Shame – Aggravation – Infatuation – Shock – Embarrassment – Restlessness – Concern – Panic – Grumpiness – Trust – Disgrace – Awkwardness – Liking – Nervousness – Exasperation – Attraction – Disorientation – Neglect – Frustration

2. When something negative happens, our brains are designed to tell us a story that keeps us safe. When we embrace the story, it affects our thinking and behavior. Ask yourself: What am I thinking? What's the consistent thought process in my head? What story am I telling myself about my future? My destiny? My ability to get back up? Name the lie. What lie am I believing?
Am I saying, "I am not (*blank*) enough?" What story am I telling myself?

_____

_____

_____

Note: Avoid comparing your suffering to someone else's. Comparative suffering helps no one.

Example of comparative suffering: One person says, "I just got fired after fifteen years of being on the job." Another person says, "That's nothing. I got just divorced after twenty-five years of marriage." Another person says, "That's nothing. My child just died in a car accident." Who does it help to compare painful situations like these? It's not a contest. Each person experiences pain in their own way, and all miseries are equally valid.

3. Rewrite the story by using virtue phrases like those listed below and incorporating your values and your mission.

Virtue Phrases – building blocks of character

Embracing the reality of life on its own terms	Willingness to take responsibility for every choice	Seeing the beauty in life	Speaking one's belief with a peaceable certainty
Showing attention to things and people that matter to us	Having a certainty and confidence after discerning what's right	Possessing a generous heart toward those suffering	Looking for the good in every situation
Deep empathy for the less fortunate	Feeling capable and certain	Carefully thinking about the needs of others	Working together for the benefit of the collective
Using fear to fuel determination	Using inspiration to ignite our originality	Being firm when deciding or taking a stand	Experiencing our emotions without giving them control over our actions
Using the power of focus to drive our ambitions	Having a sense of personal worth and respect	Showing extreme care and attention to our work	Subduing the desire to rush decisions
Putting ourselves in someone else's shoes	Withstanding adversity and hardship	Showing the ability to adapt to change amidst stressful times	Letting go of resentments
Deeply respecting what's true and right	Being oriented toward a better world	Possessing modesty and being unpretentious	Seeing what's possible and working to make a difference
Practicing fairness in all we do	Steadfast commitment to ideals and people we care about	Being reflective and consciously aware of our actions	Keeping things where they belong
Trusting the process	Possessing the strength to recover from adversity	Being content with the basic gifts of life	Accepting personal differences and avoiding passing judgment
Seeking comprehension of the full truth	Choosing the right path at the right time	Passion for what we care about	Treating others with honor
Pursuing a goal, a person, or a belief wholeheartedly			

Example:
"I might not have gone to school for this, so I will use the power of focus to drive my pursuit of information that is relevant to serving my community and fulfilling my mission: to provide quality mentoring tools to underserved, under-resourced, and vulnerable communities in ways that support sustained social change, restore hope, and provide an avenue to mental and emotional health. I am anchored by my faith and constant pursuit of personal development. I don't care if I fail as long as I did everything I could to succeed."

_____

_____

_____

Statements of Resilience

- I might have made a mistake, but I am not a mistake.
- I might have done what they said I did, but I am not what they say I am.
- My failure or struggle will not become my identity.
- I don't care if I fail, as long as I did everything I could to succeed.
- I am not ashamed of what happened to me. I am ashamed that I was ashamed. I did nothing wrong.

Here's my favorite Bible verse regarding shame:

> *Do you see what this means—all these pioneers who blazed the way, all these veterans cheering us on? It means we'd better get on with it. Strip down, start running—and never quit! No extra spiritual fat, no parasitic sins. Keep your eyes on Jesus, who both began and finished this race we're in. Study how he did it. Because he never lost sight of where he was headed— that exhilarating finish in and with God—he could put up with anything along the way: Cross, shame, whatever. And now he's there, in the place of honor, right alongside God. When you find yourselves flagging in your faith,*

go over that story again, item by item, that long litany of hostility he plowed through. That will shoot adrenaline into your souls!
Hebrews 12:1-3, MSG

Develop an Unassailable Character

Always let others see you behaving properly, even though they may still accuse you of doing wrong. Then on the day of judgment, they will honor God by telling the good things they saw you do.
1 Peter 2:12, CEV

Cultivating character requires that you acknowledge the wrong ways of living and choose to change your life for the better (See Chapter 15). The way of character requires that you self-assess and self-confront.

In order to change your life, you have to change your lifestyle. There's a spiritual teaching that says all things are permissible, but not everything is beneficial (1 Corinthians 10:23, NIV). In other words, you may have the freedom to do anything morally permissible, but there are some things that are just not wise. For me, drinking is one of them. I made a choice not to drink, not only as a result of getting arrested but because I know it would not be wise for me in the long term.

Something might be your right, but not the most constructive thing to do. The question we have to ask ourselves is not whether something is good or bad but whether it's better or best. Remember that everything matters when it comes to character. When you think about how the little things impact the big things, you'll begin to conclude that there are no little things. Leaders and successful people understand that on the road to building a strong character, everything matters.

Maybe you don't like the kind of man or woman you have become. The good news is you can change. Here are some questions to help search for cracks in your character so that you can self-assess and if need be, self-confront.

The longer cracks in your character go unaddressed, the deeper they become.

WHO TAUGHT YOU TO LOVE?

What parts of your character do you need to address?

1. Are you judgmental and critical of others instead of someone who provides constructive feedback?
Note: Let the one who has never sinned throw the first stone! (John 8:7, NLT).
It is very easy to judge another person's weakness by your strength in that area. But we are all weak in some area of our life.

2. Do you gossip about other people or do you keep confidences shared with you? The definition of gossip is bearing bad news behind someone's back.
Note: A gossip betrays a confidence; so avoid anyone who talks too much. (Proverbs 20:19, NIV).

3. Are you lazy or do you spend time working on activities that can benefit you and the community?
Note: Lazy hands make for poverty, but diligent hands bring wealth. (Proverbs 10:4, NIV)

4. Do you hold on to grudges and find ways to get revenge on others instead of forgiving others and gaining wisdom from the experience?
Note: Get rid of all bitterness, rage and anger, brawling and slander, along with every form of malice. Be kind and compassionate to one another, forgiving each other, just as in Christ God forgave you. (Ephesian 4:31-32, NIV).

5. Do you have any unhealthy habits or addictions that you need to stop? Have you found ways to get help in dealing with your issues, like attending a support group or seeing counselor?
Note: You say, "I am allowed to do anything"—but not everything is good for you. And even though "I am allowed to do anything," I must not become a slave to anything. (1 Corinthians 6:12, NLT).
An addiction is meeting a legitimate need in an illegitimate way. It's only an addiction if you want to stop.

6. Do you listen to music, watch movies or shows, or visit websites that offer mostly negative content that will not help you to be wiser, more thoughtful, or better as a person?
Thought: "Summing it all up, friends, I'd say you'll do best by filling your minds and meditating on things true, noble, reputable, authentic, compelling, gracious—the best, not the worst; the beautiful, not the ugly; things to praise, not things to curse. Put into practice what you learned from me, what you heard and saw and realized. Do that, and God, who makes everything work together, will work you into his most excellent harmonies" (Philippians 4:8-9, MSG). You become what you think about. Garbage in, garbage out.

7. What kind of place would this world be if everybody in it was just like you? What if everyone worked like you or served like you or thought like you or forgave like you? Would the world be better or worse as a result?

8. Are you a person of your word? Can people count on you to following through what you say or do you just talk about what you will do with no follow-through?
Verse: "Like clouds and wind without rain is one who boasts of gifts never given" (Proverbs 25:14, NIV).

Let this be a time when you can be honest with yourself. What's done in the dark will come to the light. At the end of the day, the smartest thing to do is the right thing, especially at the beginning. It's hard to confront your own hypocrisy. Bring it into the light while the consequences of a poor character are minimal, because the longer cracks in your character go unaddressed, the deeper and more destructive they get. This doesn't need to be something you share with people, although finding a safe and trusted friend or counselor may be helpful. It's a tool for you to begin to ask yourself the hard questions about your character before it adversely affects your life and the lives of others. As a leader, you want to not only start well, but you want to finish well.

One of the end goals for everyone's life is to be scandal-free, particularly in three areas: power, money, and sex. These are big areas of temptation that can derail anyone from doing great things. I believe everyone needs to be acquainted with their moral weakness and put boundaries in place to protect them from themselves.

Some people who try to rush themselves on the journey to success might be doing a disservice to their calling. They might be ready for the success they achieve, but not the temptation that will come with that success. You must fear your own strength and capabilities when they are used without reflection. That's why constant repetition and meditation on your purpose is important, so your actions will be rooted in being centered and in a good mental and emotional space. To achieve the discipline of building character, we must devote time to acquiring knowledge and adequate attention to apply it to our lives, both public and private. Not everyone is going to have the same level of talent, but we can all choose to have consistency of character. Just like any muscle, it you don't use it, you will lose it. Make character reflection part of your daily regimen.

3 The Battle People Know Nothing About – We Must Acknowledge the Wounds That Can't be Seen

There's a popular saying: "Be kind to everyone you meet because they may be fighting a battle you know nothing about." If each generation is responsible for being more ethical than the previous generation, then we can be proactive enough to understand what burdens people are carrying.

Safe communities don't allow people to be dehumanized, degraded, and demoralized in the name of culture. Some cultures have insensitive and unsympathetic people who only look through the lens of their experience. When people haven't been through what you've been through, they tend to be less sensitive. Their advice is corrupted by the arrogance of their inexperience. Other cultures have ignorant people who need to be informed.

Phrases like, *"When I was coming up…" "The way we did things…" "This generation.."*, can signal a dismissive spirit that creates a lack of safety and causes alienation. Some foundational lessons come from intergenerational wisdom, but there are also negative legacies and pathologies that went unacknowledged and need to be healed. Contrary to popular belief, time does not heal all wounds, and healing isn't linear.

It's not uncommon for someone to have been well-adjusted, functional, even thriving in life and then be triggered by a past experience and be thrown into an emotional and psychological limbo, disorientation, and destabilization.

If we are going to do better at loving one another, we must recognize that we need more than courage to heal. We need safety, which includes empathy and compassion. Without that, any form of healing will be through a form of counterfeit safety.

One of the greatest things that stops people from stepping out to pursue their goals is *shame*, the feeling of being unloved and defective. If we are shaming people, then we are the greatest problem and can provide the greatest solution.

The general public is familiar with the fallout of family breakdown rooted in abuse and neglect, but they might not be intimately aware of the long-term effects on the lives of those affected.

It's been said that a wound needs a witness. When you don't bring your problems to people, oftentimes people begin to believe you don't have any. As such, it's vitally important that we take the teachings seriously, because the pain that's not transformed will be transmitted. Your community might not have the emotional capacity or the tools to handle your pain, but it is possible to grow in understanding and empathy.

There's a version of people that we want to see, but we can't know whether it's accurate until we learn their stories. We need to create a high-resolution picture of two of the most important issues / open secrets that affect people and their loved ones deeply:

Childhood sexual abuse p.102-105

Fatherlessness p.106-112

I will provide a point of reference to give you an on-ramp to understanding these issues.

What Being Molested Can Cost Someone

Sexual abuse is unwanted sexual activity, with perpetrators using force, making threats, or taking advantage of victims not able to give consent. According to child advocacy experts, about one in six boys and one in four girls are sexually abused before the age of eighteen. According to my conversations with social workers and therapists, the numbers are probably higher. Many people choose to not report abuse out of shame and fear.

Part of the process of healing is having your pain validated. These childhood wounds affect adult decisions in relationships, career, and finances. I've seen these issues up close and personal from the many people who have been courageous enough to share their stories with the world.

Many times, the language of abuse gets sanitized. People might want to know what happened and how it has affected you. So here's a concise description of the losses that result from childhood sexual abuse. These losses can't be easily seen, but they deserve serious attention.

The cost to a child who gets molested is higher than most people may know or choose to acknowledge. It's too easy to dismiss or minimize the damage by saying, "It's pretty common," or "Get over it." Abuse affects a person in many ways that may be difficult for some to understand. These losses can first appear many years after the abuse took place.

- It can cost your childhood. Repeated molestation can leave you feeling betrayed, abandoned, and constantly tyrannized by the pain of emotional isolation and secret-keeping.
- It can cost the ability to trust people. When you've been abused, you might begin to see people as reckless takers and exploiters who only look at you through the lens of their agenda. It can also make you trust people who are unreliable.
- It can cost your ability to depend on authority figures. If the people in power were not aware of your abuse, you might begin to question every decision made by those in authority out of anger at their ignorance and resentment for your pain.
- It can cost you your spontaneity. I recognized that I was emotionally bleeding, and it was a nuisance to some people, so I would keep a distance from others and avoid events where there would be large groups of people.
- It can cost your belief in something greater. When you go through pain that you can't understood, you question the legitimacy of every worldview you've been given.

- It can cost your academic achievement. Being molested can affect your mental focus. The flood of emotions can keep you from applying yourself fully to the task at hand.
- It can cost you clarity of identity. A sexual and emotional confusion can occur. For some, the confusion leads to dangerous experimentation or an emotional numbing, both of which cause other problems.
- It can cost time. You can start running from the pain of the experience and anything that reminds you of the experience, and that can become a full-time process.
- It can cost your family. You may go through emotional turmoil that robs you of the potential to have a healthy family life. You might act out in unpredictable ways that can cost you your family, and maybe even your freedom.

Healing is possible, which I know personally. But you need to know that sexual abuse is not a "get over it" thing. It's an evil thief whose damage goes deep and keeps taking until we can face it and start to heal.

There was life before the trauma and there will be life after the trauma. Healing is available if you are courageous enough to do the work. What you've been through is an indication of the wounds that need to be healed and the lessons that need to be learned on how to heal. Some wounds, if not dealt with properly, can make people bitter, caustic, angry, and poisonous.

Here are a couple things I recommend:

1. **Heal the mind.** Ask yourself the hard questions about what negative thinking styles and unhealthy habits or addictions you've adopted. Review the **Survivor or Victim** assessment at the end of this section. Get informed. Below you'll find several resources that have been a benefit to me and many others. Please take the step. Recovery requires that you pick up the pieces of the past so that you can see yourself more completely and enjoy a freedom to make choices that are not determined by what happened to you.
2. **Heal the heart.** Break the silence. I know this statement is a recurring

theme. We are as sick as the secrets we keep. For some people, simply speaking to a safe person about their experience is all that is needed. What's common among sexual abuse survivors is the feeling of being alone. For all survivors, I want you to know that you're not alone. See the section **Make Sure the Pearls are Safe Here – Cultivate Goodness From the Inside Out** to know how to evaluate *safe* people to talk to. For others, they need to work through the healing process. See the resources below to find the next steps. Healing happens in the valley, not the mountaintop. Find supportive, skilled, and trusted help. It could be a support group or a therapist. See the Appendix *on* ***Choosing a Counselor***.

3. **Hurt people hurt people. Healed people heal people.** I believe that once you start to get healing from the pain of your past, your purpose will begin to reveal itself. It can help to further your healing and change someone else's life. Adopt a mindset that you will help other people with what you've learned. You can redeem your pain by turning it into a means of serving your community and the world. Make a choice to positively evaluate your past experience and use it as a stepping stone instead of a deterrent to your calling.

Recommended Resources

These can be found on www.amazon.com, www.audible.com, or your local Barnes & Noble.

Book: *Courage to Heal* by Laura Davis
Book: *Beyond Betrayal* by Richard B. Gartner
Book: *Victims No Longer* by Mike Lew
Book: *Uncaged Project* by Sallie Culbreth M.A. and Anne Quinn
Book: *When A Man You Love Was Abused* by Cecil Murphey
Book: *Not Quite Healed* by Cecil Murphey
Book: *I Thought It Was Just Me* by Brene Brown
DVD: *Boys & Men Healing from Child Sexual Abuse*
DVD: *The Healing Years – A Documentary About Surviving Incest and Child Sexual Abuse*

Fatherlessness: Heal the Hole in Your Soul

My father worked a lot when I was growing up. He was a hard worker who provided for his family but didn't have much time to come to my extracurricular activities. I played basketball in high school. I remember a game that my father came to. I saw him arrive. Ironically, I was being substituted into the game just as he walked in. The referee blew the whistle. My teammate inbounded the ball to the point guard and the point guard passed it to me.

The way the play was set up, I was supposed to pass the ball back to the point guard. In my head, I said, "No thanks coach. You can bench me for the rest of the season, but I have to show my dad I can play." This was my opportunity to show my dad that I was good, I knew how to play, and even more importantly, that I had value. I drove to the basket like there was no tomorrow. I jumped as high as I could, like I was Dwayne Wade with a resolve to score. I scored! had two points for the whole game.

My coach took me out, but it was complete. My dad knew I could play. That one moment was cemented in my heart and mind forever. It highlighted the power of a father's approval and a child's desire to prove their worth and value. Fathers are able to make emotional investments in children from which those children can withdraw for the rest of their lives.

That day boosted my self-esteem and I walked with a little more confidence. It sounds silly, but it is amazing to me how motivating and empowering a father's approval is to a child. Kids just want to know they are wanted, that they have value, that they matter, and that they are loved.

A child who is fatherless cannot get that validation and sense of belonging, Many times, devastating things happen as a result. Fatherlessness is plaguing our country. One in three children in America grow up without a father. The reasons for this vary. It can be due to death, divorce, or abandonment; the particular details surrounding each situation can be even more complex. No matter how it happens, the father's absence causes emotional pain and leave scars. Many times, it's not what *happens* that hurts (abuse, trauma, witnessing addiction/dysfunction in the family, etc.) but what *should have happened* or what was missing (love, appreciation, teaching boundaries, healthy praise, etc.). The pain of fatherlessness ends up manifesting itself in unhealthy ways.

What are the effects of fatherlessness?

1. **Self-esteem/self-worth issues**
   The pain of fatherless is the same, but the impact is different for sons and daughters. For sons, an absent father takes away self-esteem. Sons might never see a benchmark or barometer for manhood. For daughters, an absent father takes away self-worth. Overall, fatherlessness leaves a feeling in hearts that suggests that the child is defective or inadequate in some way. There are often patterns of insecurity, confusion, and sadness that continue through life.

2. **Relationship issues / Fear of rejection, abandonment, commitment**
   A father teaches a daughter what to expect from men. A father teaches a son how to treat women. When those lessons are not learned, many relational mistakes are made.

   One young man told me that his standard of how to treat women came from what he saw in movies and TV shows. In light of what's on TV these days, that's pretty scary. One woman told me that she would not have dated half of the men she dated if she'd had a good father in her life who could show her how to spot nonsense from a mile away. Fatherless women can be left without a model for what to expect from a man. There also can be a tremendous fear of commitment, because the feeling of abandonment and rejection is known all too well. Some people sabotage their relationships because they are uncomfortable with the vulnerability of an intimate relationship, or they leave abruptly because it's better to leave than to be left. These cycles exist for men and women trying to avoid inner pain.

   I recently read a book called *Four Things Women Want From Men* by A.R. Bernard. It's written to help women establish a standard for evaluating men and to give men a framework to evaluate themselves. The premise is that when a man becomes the kind of man that a woman can respect and admire, it liberates her to be the kind of woman she was meant to be, which creates a healthy relationship. Let's commit to learning these lessons sooner rather than later to avoid much of the pain and drama that happens way too often in relationships.

In addition, you can also pick up *Who Taught You to be a Man*, which provides a structure that I hope can be used as a system of thinking and living that leads to an impactful life. These lessons were written to help you heal the destructive messages about manhood along your journey that wounded your mind, heart, and spirit. Pick up a copy at **www.the-bridge330.store**.

3. **Anger**
Fatherlessness can cause sadness and fear. These are the primary emotions, but often it also causes the secondary emotion, anger. Anger is more socially acceptable in men, but women also feel anger. It generally manifests itself in two forms: rage or depression. Unresolved feelings of anger show up as rage when the anger is externalized and depression when it's internalized. Our social media age has done a great job of capturing these moments of violence. Whenever a fight breaks out, people pull out their phone cameras instead of intervening. People have lost their outrage at the state of the violence in communities. Depression occurs when the anger becomes internalized and no healthy outlet is used for its expression.

4. **Addiction**
Every fatherless child has a hole in their soul that is the shape of their father. That hole is a void that can fill up with negative things like drugs, alcohol, overeating, overspending, etc. Youth are more at risk of substance use when they lack a highly involved father or father figure.

5. **Promiscuity/Teenage pregnancy**
Teens without fathers are twice as likely to become involved in early sexual activity and seven times as likely to get pregnant during adolescence. My experience as a social worker and my discussions with educators, therapists, and other social workers, confirm that fatherlessness plays a role in promiscuity, particularly for young girls who are left to handle the weight of the decision to be sexually active.

6. **Academic performance/Dropout rates**
Students living in fatherless homes are twice as likely to repeat a grade in school. More than half of all high school dropouts come from fatherless homes. Father involvement in a child's academic life is associated with the higher likelihood of a child staying in school and performing well

academically. A good father is there to provide the structure and discipline to keep a child on track.

Ways to Heal from and Deal with Fatherlessness

1) **Grieve**. Find safe places to acknowledge your fatherlessness and grieve the loss of your father. You might have to see yourself as a victim before you can see yourself as a survivor. You were victimized by your father's absence, and you might have been ignoring the pain it has caused. It's preferable to work on your grief in a support group or with a counselor who understands the issue of fatherlessness. Use Chapter 8 as a guide for grieving.
2) **Forgive**. Remember that your father's absence had nothing to do with you. The reasons for a father not being there can vary, but it has nothing to do with the worth or value of their children. You might need to forgive your absent parent, but absolve yourself from guilt. You can become a survivor. See Chapter 7 on Forgiveness, and the end of this section on how to be a survivor.
3) **Achieve**. Be the best person you can be, in spite of not having your father. Identify the deficits of fatherlessness in your life and put things in place to deal with what you didn't get. For example, if you never learned how to manage money, take a class on money management. If you don't have healthy relational skills, see a coach or a counselor. Books, classes, and therapy can help fill in areas of your life where you should have received guidance.
4) **Reconnect** with yourself. It's a great and important step in the healing process to learn to face yourself—both your best self and your broken self, your bold self and your bruised self. Part 1 on Self-Awareness in this book is a great starting point for discovering or rediscovering who you are.
5) **Help others**. Do the work above, and if you feel comfortable, use your experience of fatherlessness to provide the support and affirmation to others. Fatherlessness leaves a yearning for relationship. When I first started mentoring, I noticed that my mentees didn't just want

information—they wanted relationship. They wanted to talk about how their first interview went. They wanted someone to show them how to budget their money and talk about their experiences with money, not just walk them through the mechanics. Within the relationship—when people can be honest about their fears, pains, frustration, hopes, and joys—healing takes place. Some ministries have been founded by fatherless people to help give other people what they didn't get growing up. Find a way to serve as a surrogate father for someone who needs one. You can mentor and coach through a lot of different programs like Big Brothers Big Sister or the Boys & Girls Club. Go to www.bbbs.org or www.bcga.org.

For Fathers Who Want to Get Back into Their Child's Life
I empathize with fathers who have not been there for their child for many different reasons. I understand that it's hard to be what you haven't seen. Life isn't always fair, and it's truly not always your fault.

Many men who leave their families come from fatherless homes and eventually succumb to the fear of not being able to be a good father. A difficult relationship with their child's mother can make it almost impossible for a father to see his child. I write this not to beat you up or to berate you, but to encourage you to take the opportunity to get back into the life of your child—even if you have to fight for it using every legal and emotionally healthy avenue available. Stay in touch with your child and if possible, with the child's mother.

Our society sometimes sees the role of the father as providing financial support, but being a father is more than that. Being a father is about nurturing, guiding, protecting, and building up. It's not about the *presents* but the *presence*. At the end of this chapter, I will share some resources to help support you as you prepare to re-enter the life of your child.

These action steps can serve as an on-ramp to get back on the road to a wholesome relationship with your child:

Action Steps for Reconnection

1) **Forgive your mistakes**. Give yourself the space to honor your mistakes and their consequences, as well as your separation from your child. We are not perfect people, but mistakes don't define you. Grieve them and forgive yourself so you can get on to the work of reconnecting with your child. See Chapters 7 and 8 on Grieving and Forgiveness.

2) **Take responsibility**. Be ready to acknowledge your role in creating the problem, so you can learn how to pick up the pieces. Don't beat yourself, but do take time and effort to seriously take responsibility for the damage that was done.

3) **Manage your anger**. Find a safe place to work through your anger around the circumstances of your separation from your child. You need to talk about the portions of the situation that were not your fault, or you risk becoming depressed or letting your anger lead you to make unwise choices. A support group, a wise and trustworthy friend, or a professional counselor can help you work through your own pain and anger over becoming disconnected from your child.

4) **Stay connected**. If the communication lines are open, seek out the opportunity to speak with and if possible, be with your child. If distance is an issue, use technology that allows you to see your child while you communicate. Be careful about what you promise to do during these conversations, because children will take every word seriously.

5) **Demonstrate your love**. Tell your child that you love them, but also reinforce your words with actions. Be consistent, to help establish a foundation of trust. You have to work to understand that your child also might be frustrated with the situation. Try to learn about the person they've become without you, so that you can support the person they will become with you there.

6) **Continue to grow**. Focus on your own growth and development, because you cannot give what you don't have. See Part 3 on *Safe Communities Launch People Into their Destinies* for a good place to start. You cannot give what you don't have. Begin to develop your sense of self and build on it.

Recommended Resources

These books can be found on www.amazon.com, www.audible.com, or your local Barnes & Noble.

Fatherless Sons – Healing the Legacy of Loss by Jonathan Diamond, PhD
Whatever Happened to Daddy's Little Girl? By Jonetta Rose Barras
The Fatherless Daughter Project: Understanding Our Losses and Reclaiming Our Lives by Denna D. Babul and Karin Luise
Being The Dad I Never Had: Lifelong Lessons For Fathering After Fatherlessness by Dr. David R. Inniss

Survivor or Victim

A man crossing the street was suddenly struck by a speeding, drunk driver. He survived with serious injuries. Doctors assumed that the man would never be able to walk again.

The man had a wife and two daughters. He wept, picturing everything he would lose now: the ability to play sports, to walk his daughter down the aisle, and even to work to support his family. After many hours of crying, he realized that he might not have been responsible for what happened to him—but he was responsible for what happened next.

The accident was a drunk driver's fault, but the healing and recovery were up to him. He could schedule physical therapy appointments and arrange for someone to transport him to and from the doctor. He could organize his life to be as productive as possible. While he had a great support system, his healing was his responsibility.

Instead of being a victim, he became a survivor, someone who functions and even prospers in spite of hardship. He chose not to remain helpless and hopeless.

When tough times hit, what mindset do you take on? Are you a survivor or a victim? How do you know which you are?

Nine Signs You Are a Victim

1) You complain rather than take action to improve your situation.
2) You discuss the same issues over and over, month after month, and sometimes year after year.
3) You receive solutions but always seem to find them unworkable or inapplicable to your circumstance.
4) You wait for a "superman" to rescue you.
5) You avoid taking responsibility for your actions. You look for people or circumstances to blame for your current condition.
6) You are a parasite. You take but don't give. You're more of a liability than an asset because of your selfish perspective.
7) You refuse to take care of yourself, to ensure that someone else will have to take care of you.
8) You are constantly in "trouble" because you catastrophize situations.
9) You drain the people around you with your unwillingness to deal with your situations head on.

Nine Signs You Are a Survivor

1) You engage in behaviors to move you in the direction of improving your situation and restoring your sense of hope.
2) You are willing to fight the fear of change and make sacrifices to position yourself to grow.
3) You are patient because you understand that delayed gratification is a tool on your journey to reach your goal.
4) You fight your fears on a daily basis.
5) You make plans based on reality, not a fantasy world.
6) You embrace your circumstances instead of running from them.
7) You use all the resources at your disposal to bring about positive change.
8) You seek skilled help when you get stuck instead of spinning your wheels.
9) You stay prudent instead of being impulsive and reacting solely off emotion.

Part 3

Safe Communities Launch People Into their Destinies—*You Have Purpose*

**When David had served God's purposes
during his lifetime, he fell asleep.
Acts 13:36, NCB**

The greatest disaster is not dying young. It's not serving your purpose for this generation. Unfortunately, we live in a world that nurtures ambitions rooted in selfishness, economic necessity, and short-term profit maximization. In short, our world wants us to focus on currency and not legacy.

One's calling in life includes a task of responsibility (purpose) directed at problems that you are personally fulfilled by addressing.

Every person knows, deep inside, what their purpose is. Unfortunately, most people haven't taken the time to discover what it is. Journaling is an underutilized tool on the road to finding your purpose.

Every thirty, sixty, or ninety days, you will want to review what their days have been like and identify consistent themes.

Recollection is likely to turn up some useful information. There are clues in your history that can speak to your destiny. Finding your purpose is often not a discovery but a recovery of themes from your past.

One of the goals of life should be to identify your deeply felt desires and values and how they align with the needs you see in the world. The time that this exercise requires is so small and so minimal compared to what's at stake: spending the rest of your life clueless about why you are here.

Here's a list of questions that you can use to grow in awareness of your purpose.

Anger—What makes you mad?
Your greatest frustration is a problem you are here to solve.

Sadness—What makes you sad?
Ask the Lord to break your heart with what breaks his heart.

Passion—What makes you excited?
Don't do things that you think the world needs. Do the things that bring you to life, because the world needs people who are fully alive.

Fear—What makes you afraid?
What would your life look like if you were not afraid? Name your fears and fight them.

WHO TAUGHT YOU TO LOVE?

Through my constant reflection and journaling over several years, here are some of the issues that emerged from asking myself these questions, which served as a catalyst for **TheBridge330 Mentoring Program**:

- One in three children in America grow up fatherless
- One in three girls, and one in six boys will experience childhood sexual abuse, according to child advocacy experts
- One in three black boys will go to jail or prison in their lifetime
- An average of 10,000 people are released from American prisons each week
- The average net worth of a black family in NJ is $5,900; for a white family, the number is $309,000
- The leading cause of death of black men under age forty-four is homicide
- The Innocence Project reports 2 to 5 percent of people behind bars—approximately 40,000 to 100,000 people—are innocent.
- As of 2020, there are 580,000 people experiencing homelessness in America.

Safe communities encourage uniqueness and provide tried and true principles to encourage success and manifestation of purpose. In my opinion, many of the problems in our communities cannot be solved by money; people also need healthy relationships, where others inspire and facilitate hope, healing, compassion, and empathy through the example of their own lives. I certainly have not arrived in living these lessons out entirely. I have come to realize that there's always more to learn and to heal from. But we need to continually learn from and apply these foundational lessons.

It's been said that we can't be courageous in a big world unless we have a small world where we can work through our pain and fears. It's also true that we can only reach our destiny in a world where we can take time to become aware of the essential raw materials of destiny.

In order to make purposeful decisions, you need certain habits, practices, and disciplines. There are five words that I believe are essential to understand as it relates to purpose: time, business, friendship, dreams, and code.

Five words to consider as you ponder your life purpose:

Time – Chapter 10

> *Teach us to comprehend how few our days are so that our hearts may be filled with wisdom.* Psalm 90:12, NCB
> *Look carefully then how you walk! Live purposefully and worthily and accurately, not as the unwise and witless, but as wise (sensible, intelligent people). Making the very most of the time [buying up each opportunity], because the days are evil.* Ephesians 5:15-16, AMPC

What you do in the free hours can either free you or enslave you.

Business – Chapter 11

> *Try your best to live quietly, to mind your own business, and to work hard.* 1 Thessalonians 4:11, CEV

The word *"business"* is anything that requires deliberate activity requiring time and effort. Part of this Scripture's warning is to avoid frivolous or unnecessary preoccupations.

Friendship – Chapter 12

> *Godly people are careful about the friends they choose. But the way of sinners leads them down the wrong path.* Proverbs 12:26, NIRV
> *You might call many people your "friends," but it is hard to find someone who can really be trusted.* Proverbs 20:6, ERV

Choose association based on your destination. True friendships are those who mutually respect and nurture each other's God-given purpose.

Dream – Chapter 13

Hope deferred makes the heart sick; but when dreams come true at last, there is life and joy. Proverbs 13:12, TLB

Real pleasure doesn't come from worldly pursuits. Real pleasure comes from bringing your dreams to fruition.

Code – Chapter 14

Whoever obeys a commandment keeps himself safe, but someone who is contemptuous in conduct will die. Proverbs 19:16, ISV

Everyone wants to change the world; no one wants to change themselves. The world would be a better place if everyone looked in the mirror before they cast judgment.

– 10 –

Who Are You? and What Time Is It?: Know What Season of Life You're In

Work on Your Self-Awareness: You cannot be the best version of yourself if you don't know yourself.

This section will give you a framework to develop a conscious knowledge of how you're wired: your calling, talents, your dreams and visions, your values, your tribe, your ideal work style, and your beliefs. Growing in self-awareness is like digging for gold. How many tools should we use to find the gold of our authentic selves? As many as we can find.

Getting to know yourself is one of the most difficult things to do but one of the most rewarding. It's going to take intentionality, time, focus, effort, perseverance, and tenacity. The benefits of these tools will far outweigh the time and effort put into the work. Part of the journey of creating a life directed toward purpose requires mindful awareness and deliberate attention to our makeup, thoughts, emotions, and experiences. One thing I've observed, over time, is that the people who live wholeheartedly and love their work played a significant role in designing their life's path and creating the work they love. The foundation of their fulfillment was self-awareness. A byproduct of knowing who you are will be the knowledge of what you want. That's how you can wake up every day and love what you do. To get there, you have to commit yourself to doing the work as often, and as much, as necessary.

I want to share an email exchange with one of my college professors from over a decade ago, to set the stage as to why self-awareness is important.

Jonathan:
We have spoken in the past about your interest in teaching. I would like to talk to you about the opportunity at a local school in Newark, NJ.

It would offer you the opportunity to see if you like teaching. Given your knowledge of Newark and your success in high school and college – Jonathan, this is a real opportunity to make a difference in the lives of others.

My response:
I would like to know if I can meet with you to discuss this opportunity. There are several things that may keep me from pursuing it and I would like to have your insight.

Response:
Jonathan – Sure on all accounts. I hear that you have a very nice job offer already. The hardest choices are when you have to choose between two or more good things. Nonetheless, offer God gratitude for the blessings of such choices.

After much reflection and unnecessary pain, I can say that I made a misguided choice. My values and motivations were externally derived instead of personally discovered. At the time, I thought I was doing the right thing. I was chasing money, social acceptance, and family approval. In the process, I betrayed one of my deepest values, which is service to my community and love for learning and facilitating learning for others. I dishonored myself by settling for a life that didn't serve my highest and best use.

However, no experience is wasted if lessons are learned, especially if those lessons are shared. I know that I'm not alone in making major life choices with poor self-awareness, misguided values, and the lack of courage to displease people who had agendas for my life that conflicted with a regard for my well-being. They might have meant well, but their counsel didn't serve me well. I was and am ultimately responsible for my choices and have no one to hold accountable but me. Though I managed to be relatively successful in my career, there were many parts of the journey where I felt weird, out of place, and downright miserable.

My hope is that what made me weird in those moments made me unique at this moment.

Below is a list of the tools needed to create and execute a life plan. I refer to them as **Reflection Tools**. Chapter references are from *Bridge the Gaps – Lessons on Self-Awareness, Self-Development, and Self-Care*:

1. **Finding out how you're wired:** Don't ask yourself what the world needs. Ask yourself what makes you come alive, because what the world needs is people who have come alive. (Chapter 1)
2. **Learning to be real**: To be yourself in a world that is constantly trying to make you something else is the greatest accomplishment. (Chapter 2)
3. **Finding out what's important to you?:** What do you want most, versus what you want now? (Chapter 3)
4. **Finding what you're good at:** People who fulfill their calling exude a connection to their gift that transcends the recognition they receive. (Chapter 4)
5. **Community feedback:** You can't see the picture when you're in the frame. (Chapter 5)
6. **Learning how you work best:** You can't judge a fish by its ability to climb a tree. (Chapter 6)
7. **Finding out what you believe:** To be nobody but yourself in a world which is doing its best, night and day, to make you everybody else means to fight the hardest battle which any human being can fight, and never stop fighting. (Chapter 7)
8. **Learning how to dream:** We overestimate what we can do in a year and underestimate what we can do in ten years. (Chapter 8)
9. **Learning from the best:** You have to choose the right heroes. (Chapter 9)
10. **Learning how to trust the process:** You don't have to be perfect, but you must be faithful. (Chapter 10)

What Time Is it?

Some say life is about trying to beat the odds. Others say it's about dog-eat-dog competition and warfare with enemies trying to destroy you. The truth is that life is a journey with different seasons.
Know which season you're in—so you'll know how to dress.

WHO TAUGHT YOU TO LOVE?

Take a moment to read and reflect on the following popular passage from the book of Ecclesiastes:

For everything[a] there is an appointed time, and an appropriate time for every activity on earth:
A time to be born, and a time to die; a time to plant, and a time to uproot what was planted.
A time to kill, and a time to heal; a time to break down, and a time to build up.
A time to weep, and a time to laugh; a time to mourn, and a time to dance.
A time to throw away stones, and a time to gather stones; a time to embrace, and a time to refrain from embracing.
A time to search, and a time to give something up as lost;[b] a time to keep, and a time to throw away.
A time to rip, and a time to sew; a time to keep silent, and a time to speak.
A time to love, and a time to hate; a time for war, and a time for peace.
Ecclesiastes 3, NET

I believe it's best to have one major focus in life. Having a single focus will help to keep you on task. This chapter is extremely important, because the thing that matters most in your personal development might not always get the attention it deserves. You need intentionality, and that comes with singular focus. Trying to do two things with maximum effort is like trying to chase two rabbits. Both will get away.

Get comfortable with the fact that some things will have to wait for your attention. Your aim is to focus on what needs to be accomplished *now* and what perspective you need to cultivate *in this season*. Life will be much simpler and less hectic once you know your primary goal. Most people who went on to accomplish great things identified a sole focus and held on with relentless tenacity.

Geoffrey Canada's primary focus was to provide comprehensive educational services to poor minority children from the cradle to college in Harlem, NY. He is a black, anti-poverty, education reform advocate and founder of the Harlem Children's Zone, a pioneering nonprofit organization committed to ending generational poverty. His organization has served more than 10,000 children for more than thirty years.

Bryan Stevenson's primary focus was to help innocent people, largely black and poor, obtain appropriate legal assistance. He is the founder of Equal Justice Initiative, a nonprofit organization that works to end mass incarceration, excessive punishment, and racial inequality. Mr. Stevenson and his staff have won reversals, relief, or release from prison for more than 135 wrongly condemned prisoners on death row and have won relief for hundreds of others wrongly convicted or unfairly sentenced.

Mother Theresa's primary focus was to help the homeless people outside of her convent learn to read and write.
Mother Teresa demonstrated her differentiation with her request for exclaustration—a release from her vows—so she could better serve the poor of Calcutta, India. She later started a hospice for those who were sick and dying on the streets and became a global figure for service and charity.

Not everyone will find the same kind of early clarity about their purpose. Many of us stumble before we find that main focus. As you grow in self-awareness, prioritizing will get easier (see below).

In this season of my life, my focus is writing books to begin conversations that can promote positive change. My goal is to ignite hope and bring healing to my community. It has taken time for me to build the skillset, resources, and confidence to feel comfortable pursuing this goal. Like all of us, my life is a work in progress.

When I was in high school, I heard a motivational speaker say something that changed my life forever: "If you want to hide something from a black man, put it in a book." This speaker made the statement to help me and my classmates—kids in a predominantly black school—become aware of the social perception of black people in America. I felt offended, sad, and angry all at once when I heard those words. He described how the enslaved Africans were killed for learning how to read. Like many modern-day Americans, I did not see the value of reading. We take that opportunity for granted.

That statement sent me on a quest for book titles that would help my knowledge about the world grow. That was almost twenty years ago, and I am forever grateful that I was in school that day. The message sparked something important in me. From that day on, books have changed my life and helped me to serve my community.

I have compiled a list of thousands of book titles to study. Thinking about the information in those books keeps me excited and focused.

TheBridge330 mentoring program (**www.thebridge330.com**) focuses on three sets of tools, which correspond with different seasons of life. They are as follows:

1) **Reflection**: This is a time of soul-searching spent in contemplation, consideration, and personal study for the purpose of cultivating self-awareness (an integrated knowledge of purpose, talents, work styles, and values).

2) **Productivity**: This is a period of intentional positioning to progressively realize one's goals through the wise use of one's personal resources (talents, creativity, knowledge, work habits, persistence, confidence, contacts, money, etc.)

3) **Attentiveness** (personal): This is a time of intentional emotional healing and skill-building, which includes grieving losses, forgiving past transgressions, repairing boundaries, developing the skills of assertiveness, healing the shame, and developing emotionally healthy relationship skills. Common issues like mental illness, fatherlessness, sexual abuse, etc. receive special attention in this season. It includes developing stable life habits after difficult transitions like reentry, divorce, addiction recovery, etc.

Exercise: Identify Your Focus
Here are a few examples of focus based on the corresponding season:

Season: Reflection

- "I ran the streets when I was young because I had no family. I spent fifteen years of my life in prison. I used that time to find myself and to find my way. I might have ended up dead otherwise. It didn't have to be that way, but that's how it was, and I have to live with it. I have a year left on my sentence. By God's grace, I have a job lined up and a place to stay. My main focus is to find a way to heal the communities that I once played a part in destroying. I have a few ideas that I'm thinking about but I'm not sure yet."
(**Focus**: *Recovering One's Purpose / Redemption*)
- "I just graduated from high school. I have a few business ideas I want to do. I'm not sure if I'll go to college right away or at all. So the next steps are in the air."
(**Focus**: *Identifying One's Next Steps*)

Season: Productivity

- "I am focusing on getting out of debt. I got a credit card when I was in college, and because I never learned about money management, I ran up thousands of dollars in debt on nonsense. Now I'm working to change that so I can be financially free. I have to live frugally for now, and it's hard, but that's the sacrifice I need to make to get out of this debt in the next twelve months."
(**Focus**: *Financial stability*)
- "I want to open up a cleaning business where I can employ ten or twelve people in the next year. I've been doing all the jobs with a few people, and the demands are great, so I'm excited about the possibilities."
(**Focus**: *Entrepreneurial start-up*)

- "I got a 3.5 GPA last semester, and I want to be on the Dean's List every semester until I graduate college. So these next few years I will be focused on being the best student I can be."
  (**Focus**: *Academic achievement*)

Season: Attentiveness

- "I got divorced a year ago, and I feel like I'm starting all over again. I had to move out of my house, and now I'm doing better. I've been going to counseling weekly, going to the gym four times a week, and I'm taking one class every semester to finish up my degree. I see the light at the end of the tunnel."
  (**Focus**: *Emotional and mental well-being, health, and education after a major life transition*)
- "I struggle with an addiction, and I never went to get help. I am now going to counseling and my support group once a week. Every day is a battle, but I will never quit. I've been sober for the last four months."
  (**Focus**: *Sobriety*)

These examples show that everyone is different. Our priorities and individual challenges are different, so each person's focus must be different as well. Take some time to identify what your major focus should be at this point in your life. It might not be clear right away, so ask yourself this question early and often:

What should my focus be in this season of my life?

———————————————————————————

———————————————————————————

Message to the Reader: I'm under no illusion that life has been fair or easy for anyone, so I don't have the right to tell you what your focus should be in this season. However, you can overcome the obstacles you face and live a life of purpose. You have a purpose that you were designed to uniquely manifest. The next section will provide you with a system of thought and tools to bring your purpose to fruition.

— 11 —

Mind Your Business: Find Your Lane, Run Your Own Race, and Let Your Light Shine

The two most pivotal days of your life are the day you are born and the day you find out why.

If you've completed the last section, you've done some great work in cultivating self-awareness and a sense of the season of life you're in. Now here's the next step:

> *Try your best to live quietly, to mind your own business, and to work hard.*
> 1 Thessalonians 4:11, CEV

The word *business* here means anything that requires deliberate activity requiring time and effort and focus (the avoidance of unnecessary preoccupations). A safe community is one that puts you on the path to minding your own business. That begs the question: What should your business be?

Your first order of business is identifying Your Purpose—your highest priority and guiding principle.

As it relates to purpose, the three aspects of your business you need to get started are:

- Finding the lane that fits you, based on how you're wired
- Running your unique, authentic race
- Letting your light shine.

Find Your Lane

> *The purposes of a person's heart are deep waters, but one who has insight draws them out.*
> Proverbs 20:5, NLT

People often ask children, "What do you do want to do when you grow up?" They expect the child to name a particular professional ambition. A better question is, "What do you want your life to be about?" This question speaks to purpose.

In the world of personal development, you often hear these suggestions

- Pick your battle
- Start with the end in mind
- Define your success
- Identify your desired return on investment (ROI).

These instructions speak to specific aims or targets. But before you get too specific, it's best to start the process of finding your life's purpose by *finding your lane*.

Each person has a lane in life that they are qualified to travel. It is important to identify that lane, so we do not run the risk of making premature commitments to the wrong paths. You do not have to be too specific too soon. The journey to your specific destiny is a funnel.

Far too many people have been derailed by going down a path that they were not meant to travel. As a result, their lives become a series of poor choices, wasted time, and tons of regret. You can use the following exercises to prime the pump of your purpose.

Exercise #1: Merge your conviction with your vocation (journaling exercise)

The world doesn't revolve around you, but there *is* something you were made to do in the world.

Journaling is an underutilized tool on the road to finding your purpose. Because your purpose is applied and discerned on a day-to-day basis, recollection is likely to turn up some useful information. Your history contains clues that can speak to your destiny. Finding your purpose might mean not a discovery but a *recovery* of themes from your past.

Every thirty, sixty, or ninety days, it's a good idea to review what your days have been like and identify consistent themes.

One of the goals of your life should be to identify your deeply felt desires, values, and talents, and then see how they align with the needs you notice in the world. Spend some time thinking about this, and write about it. This requires a small time commitment, but it can make the difference between spending the rest of your life clueless about why you are here and using your life for something meaningful or even grand.

Ask yourself these questions every day as you interact with your family, friendships, workplace, or the world, to become more aware of your purpose.

1. *What makes you mad?* **Anger** is a clue. Your greatest frustration is a problem you are here to solve.
2. *What makes you sad?* **Sadness** is also a clue. Ask the Lord to break your heart with what breaks His heart.
3. *What makes you excited?* **Excitement** gives you important information. Don't do things that you think the world needs. Do the things that make you feel alive, because the world needs people who are fully alive.
4. *What makes you afraid?* **Fear** can help make you conscious of impending danger but it can also tell you which obstacles you need to overcome. What would your life look like if you were not afraid? Name your fears and how you might fight them.
5. *What makes you generous?* **Generosity** shows your readiness to serve a purpose. Where do you find yourself most generous? Note: If you find yourself giving everything to everyone until you have nothing left, see Chapter 33 – Boundaries in *Bridge the Gaps*.
6. *What do you talk about without being asked?* **Unsolicited conversation** shows what you know and care enough about to talk about.
7. *How do you handle situations that don't align with your moral compass?* **Integrity** tells you what is most important about how you see yourself.
8. *What are you challenged by, but not overwhelmed by?* **Suitability** tells you which activities are a natural match for your talents. "His yoke is easy, and his burden is light" (Matthew 11:30, NIV).
9. *Who inspires you?* **Role models** show us what we can see of ourselves in others.
10. *What gives you hope?* **Hope** is the conviction that doing the work makes sense, regardless of how it turns out. Where do you see possibilities while others see hopelessness and despair? Your hope is a gauge of how resilient you will be.

What is your dream? Your **dream** is the best situation you can imagine, including your dream job, dream location, and dream life. Beneath your dreams are the seeds of destiny.

Exercise #2: Simplify your purpose

I believe there is power in simplicity. After you've completed Exercise #1, choose three actions from the list below to find the form of your purpose. Choose actions that resonate with you.

Question: What do you want to do?

Action words:

Build	Repair	Learn	Destroy	Teach	Fight	Overcome	Restore	Remove	Correct
Prepare	Change	Remember	Inform	Raise	Alert	Become	Resolve	Determine	Manifest
Promote	Provide	Protect	Encourage	Make	Care	Counsel	Commit	Defend	Ensure
Revive	Break down	Prevent	Instruct	Hold on	Leave behind	Avoid	Invite	Evoke	Invoke

You can add any other words you want to include.

Question: Whom do you want to help?

Choose three groups/interests/causes from the list below that you'd like to benefit from your purpose.

Groups/Interests/Causes:

Studies of culture	Business	Animal life	Social justice	Finance	Education	Travel	World history	Great inventors	Family health
Fitness	Airplanes	Faith	African American History	Music	Gospel	Mental illness	Community building	World missions	Human development
Space exploration	Law	Nutrition	Child Care	Education	Community development	Prison Reentry	Literacy	Emotional Health	Cinema

Add any other words you want to include.

Exercise #3 – Write a purpose statement

We cannot productively live in the absence of purpose. We would never start a business without a mission statement and a set of core values. So why do we often skip over identifying a purpose for our own lives?

A clearly defined purpose statement can help us chart our course with confidence and resist our need to please others. Unfortunately, many men focus on obtaining a position or material possessions. These are not necessarily bad goals, but once people obtain the position or the material possessions they sought, they lose enthusiasm. Your goals should feed your soul, so they are always fresh and exciting.

A **purpose statement** is designed to integrate who you are and what you do. It is the way you start transforming your life from a drifting generality to a meaningful specific. Combine Exercises #1 and 2 to come up with a statement of your intention. It doesn't have to be perfect, but it must be honest and grounded in reality.

Here's mine:

"To provide quality mentoring tools to underserved, under-resourced, and vulnerable communities in ways that support sustained social change, a restoration of hope, and an avenue to mental and emotional health."

The Bridge330 Mentoring Program

Here's another example:

"To fight against the stigma of mental illness in the black community by inviting people to share their stories in an authentic and safe way."

What's yours?

_____

_____

_____

The important thing to understand about your purpose is that it's dynamic. Your purpose can and should evolve, grow, and change in complexity or simplicity. I encourage you to use these journal exercises repeatedly on the road to finding and living in line with your purpose.

Run Your Own Race[11]

> *In a race everyone runs, but only one person gets first prize.*
> *So run your race to win.*
> 1 Corinthians 9:24, TLB

In a culture of constant comparison and scarcity, our job is to take full control of the individuality we were born with and develop it, without being defeated by the harshness of life.

When you run your own race, you become self-possessed, which means you've taken full ownership and responsibility for your unique, God-given personhood and refuse to be compartmentalized, incarcerated, or institutionalized by the expectations of those who have a limited perspective of you.

If there is a person who exemplifies running their race to the very end, it's one of the most prolific actors of my generation, Chadwick Boseman. He had a great movie career where he played iconic historical figures but was launched into international stardom when he played the role of T'Challa in the Marvel movie *Black Panther*. He was diagnosed with colon cancer in 2016 and battled until he passed away on August 28, 2020 at the age of forty-three.

Boseman is a man who lived on purpose. In his final speech to his alma mater, Howard University, he discussed the dilemma of the roles he played. At the beginning of his career, he was offered a six-figure job for a soap opera with a major network. During a conversation with the show's executives, who loved his previous episodes, he challenged the stereotypical role of the black character that he was auditioning for. He was fired the next day. His principles closed doors that day. With building doubt and inner conflict, he stuck to his guns, which might have paved the way for a less-stereotypical role in the future. He thought he might have been blackballed. He was knocked down, and that showed him what fight he was in. He fought back and won!

Here's a list of his works that emphasized social issues that are still relevant today.

42 (2013) – A movie about Jackie Robinson, the first African American to play in Major League Baseball. He was signed to the Brooklyn Dodgers and faced immense racism in the process.

Get On Up (2014) – A movie that describes the life of the legendary artist James Brown and ascent from poverty to superstardom.

Marshall (2017) – A biographical legal drama about the first African American Supreme Court Justice, Thurgood Marshall, who was a crusading lawyer and champion of career-defining cases.

Black Panther (2018) – A superhero movie about a leader of an independent African nation who is crowned king after his father's death. He is challenged by his long-lost cousin, who wanted the nation to abandon its isolationist practices and begin a global revolution.

21 Bridges (2019) – A movie about an embattled NYPD detective who uncovers an unexpected conspiracy while on a citywide manhunt of cop killers. The movie captures the nuances of police life.

Da 5 Bloods (2020) – A movie about the grief and emotional life of four African American veterans who served in Vietnam.

Ma Rainey's Black Bottom (2020) – A movie that depicted a black woman who refused to give her power away and used her gift to help others feel free.

Choosing your role applies to more than movie stars. Some people lose touch with who they truly are in order to play a certain role in their family, school, job, or society. To fulfill your purpose, you might have to wean yourself from the control of our social system.

One of the ways we can recognize our need for change is through our relationships and our choices. Each person is responsible for the choices he or she makes and for taking personal responsibility for his or her destiny. Each person's behavior is also significantly impacted by their environment. I try not to have an either/or perspective, but a both/and perspective. No individual has all the answers. If generational cycles (sometimes also called "generational curses") are going to be broken and patterns interrupted, it starts with your choices.

One of the ways we can recognize our need for change is through our relationships and our choices. Here's a scale that ranks how individuals act in the context of what they believe and how they interact with others. To reflect on where you are on the road to becoming true to yourself or "self-differentiated," select where you think you rank:

0 – 25

- Can't discriminate between fact and feeling
- Emotionally needy and highly reactive to others
- Much of life energy spent in winning the approval of others
- Little energy for goal-directed activities
- Can't say, "I think…" or "I believe…"
- Little emotional separation from families
- Dependent marital relationships
- Do very poorly in transitions, crises, and life adjustments
- Unable to see where they end and others begin

25– 50

- Some ability to distinguish fact and feeling
- Most of self is a "false self" and reflected from others
- When anxiety is low, they function relatively well
- Quick to imitate others and change themselves to gain acceptance from others
- Often talk one set of principles/beliefs, yet do another
- Self-esteem soars with compliments or is crushed by criticism
- Become anxious (i.e., highly reactive and "freaking out") when a relationship system falls apart or becomes unbalanced
- Often make poor decisions due to their inability to think clearly under stress
- Seek power, honor, knowledge, and love from others to clothe their false selves.

50-75

- Aware of thinking and feeling functions that work as a team
- Reasonable level of "true self"
- Can follow life goals that are determined from within
- Can state beliefs calmly without putting others down
- Marriage is a functioning partnership where intimacy can be enjoyed without losing the self
- Can allow children to progress through developmental phases into adult autonomy
- Functions well alone or with others
- Able to cope with crises without falling apart
- Stays in relational connection with others without insisting they see the world the same way

75-100 (few people function at this level)

- Are principle-oriented and goal-directed – secure in who they are, unaffected by criticism or praise
- Are able to leave family of origin and become an inner-directed, separate adult
- Sure of their beliefs but not dogmatic or closed in their thinking
- Can hear and evaluate beliefs, discarding old beliefs in favor of new ones
- Can listen without reacting and communicate without antagonizing others
- Can respect others without having to change them
- Aware of dependence on others and responsibility for others
- Free to enjoy life and play
- Able to maintain a non-anxious presence in the midst of stress and pressure
- Able to take responsibility for their own destiny

To remind yourself of your purpose, you can create a mantra to keep you grounded. Here is one that I use.

The Responsibility Mantra: *"This is my life. I'm responsible for who enters it and for what takes place in it. I determine my life mission, goals, my values, and my pace. I will respect and learn from others but my decisions for my life will be a product of my own conclusions."*

Let Your Light Shine

> *You are like that illuminating light. Let your light shine everywhere you go, that you may illumine creation, so men and women everywhere may see your good actions, may see creation at its fullest, may see your devotion to Me, and may turn and praise your Father in heaven because of it.*
> Matthew 5:16, VOICE

In a 2018 interview, Chadwick Boseman discussed his experiences of racism in South Carolina, which included being the target of racial epithets. He discussed his emotional evolution from feeling resentment to bringing unity and healing. His approach was to pray for those of ill intent and to be a light to show people where they were in error. He certainly was a light in this world.

I think his life is one that needs to be highlighted as an example of how to run your race and let your light shine to the fullest. One of his co-stars in *Da 5 Bloods*, Clarke Peters, was asked after Boseman's death what kind of man we had lost. Peters replied that he didn't think we had lost Boseman, because he had served his purpose by putting younger people on track. That had been his purpose in life, he served as a hero to many young people.

In light of Clarke's sentiment, it's fitting to say that when Boseman had "served God's purposes during his lifetime, he fell asleep" (Acts 13:36, NCB).

– 12 –

Friendship DRAFT: Have Standards/Radar for Choosing/Being Safe Friends

Godly people are careful about the friends they choose.
But the way of sinners leads them down the wrong path.
Proverbs 12:26, NIRV

You might call many people your "friends," but it is
hard to find someone who can really be trusted.
Proverbs 20:6, ERV

Most people will tell you what loyal friends
they are, but are they telling the truth?
Proverbs 20:6, TLB

In his most vulnerable moment, Jesus only had three of his twelve disciples come with him to the top of the mountain: Peter, James, and John. Friendship is what happens on the road to doing what you were called to do. Friendships require time and effort. The more friendships you have to manage, the harder it might be to stay focused on your purpose. Make sure your relationships are intentional and purposeful.

Choosing good friends is so vitally important because very few things can derail your destiny and purpose like having the wrong friends. The word "friendship" is overused and misapplied in our culture. The people who are my "friends" on social media are not friends in real life. The standard for being and choosing a friend has been broken down into the acronym DRAFT.

D – Dedicated and devoted to your well-being, not your feelings

> *A friend loves at all times, and a brother is born for a time of adversity.*
> Proverbs 17:17, NIV

Your friendships are largely determined by what's going on in your life. In some seasons of life, there may be increased connection or decreased connection. And at some points, there must be a disconnection. That is a choice that is usually difficult to make. Whether you can be friends with someone in particular seasons will be based on these factors, the **Three Ms**:

Motivation – Do they want to be friends with you because of what you provide, or just because they genuinely want to be there for you? Friendships can fail when one person feels used or slighted. Friendship requires a balance in each partner's investment, and can be derailed by a conflict of interest. In a true friendship, you are equally safe whether you fail or succeed and don't have to be concerned about their departure.

Things to Watch For:

1. "A wealthy man has many friends; the poor man has none left" (Proverbs 19:4 TLB).
   "No one has greater love [nor stronger commitment] than to lay down his own life for his friends" (John 15:13, AMP).

   Use **discernment** when choosing friends. As life circumstances change for the better, it might become less clear why people want friendship with you. Watch for patterns in people's relational habits. When do they come around or call? What is their motivation?

2. "Many people are nice to a generous person. Everyone wants to be friends with someone who gives gifts" (Proverbs 19:6, ERV).
   Some people will pretend to be your friend to abuse your giving spirit. This includes the time, talents, treasures you give. The message here is not to be less generous, but to be more discerning. Givers must set limits, because takers never do.

3. "A flattering neighbor is up to no good; he's probably planning to take advantage of you" (Proverbs 29:5, MSG).
   "Better to correct someone openly than to let him think you don't care for him at all" (Proverbs 27:5, GNT).

   "Faithful are the wounds of a friend [who corrects out of love and concern], But the kisses of an enemy are deceitful [because they serve his hidden agenda]" (Proverbs 27:6, AMP).

   Do your friends support you unconditionally but tell you the truth in a helpful way, or do they flatter you excessively? Just because someone is friendly doesn't mean they are your friend. Real friends get in your way when you're on the way down.

Maintenance – Can you handle the requirements of the relationship in this season of your life? Do you have time for the financial and emotional investment in this friendship? If you have had overall bad experiences with relationships, the intimacy is going to take longer, but it will go deeper.

Things to Watch For:

1. **Demanding boundary violators**—"Don't visit your neighbors too often, or you will wear out your welcome" (Proverbs 25:17, NLT). Invited guests are welcomed best.
2. **Unreliable**—"Trusting a double-crosser when you're in trouble is like biting down on an abscessed tooth" (Proverbs 25:19, MSG).

Maturity – Maturity means you operate in a way that is courageous and considerate. Is your friend able to understand your needs, your perspective, and your season of life—and vice versa—so that there is reciprocity? A difference in your views about religion, politics, or life in general can lead to tensions and frustrations. Relationships cannot last with repeated failures in the department of empathy. See the section on Agreement and Edification

Things to watch for:

1. "Jonathan said to him, 'Don't be afraid! My father Saul's hand won't touch you. You will be king over Israel, and I will be your second in command. Even my father Saul knows this'" (1 Samuel 23:17).
   True friends are not afraid of your elevation in life. One of the signs of spiritual maturity and development is to be able to delight in the success of your neighbor.
2. "Don't hang out with angry people; don't keep company with hotheads. Bad temper is contagious— don't get infected" (Proverbs 22:24, MSG). A friend who is impulsive or angry will not be a helper on your path.

Reflection Questions

1. Have you always been a good friend? This is a tough question. Maturity says that you "take the log out of your eye, and then you'll see clearly to take the splinter out of your brother's or sister's eye" (Matthew 7:5, CEB).
2. The maturity of the relationship is determined by your ability to have

uncomfortable conversations. If you have a relationship where you don't want to talk about the hard stuff, the relationship has lost its intimacy. You shouldn't be afraid to rock the boat, especially when the boat is sinking.

R – *Respectful of your boundaries*
Boundaries represent what you are and are not responsible for, and what is appropriate behavior in relationships. In detoxing the generational baggage of the common family dynamics that exist, one area to explore and rebuild is in the area of boundaries.

Unsolicited advice robs people of the initiative needed to become independent and self-determined, thereby reducing the opportunity for vulnerability they need to become self-possessed. Unsolicited advice is also disrespectful and can be interpreted as a lack of faith in the person receiving the advice. In order to effectively fulfill your purpose, one must continually cultivate self-differentiation and mental toughness. See ***Chapter 11 – Mind Your Business: Find Your Lane, Run Your Own Race, and Let Your Light Shine.***

Things to Watch For:

1. "You may suffer, but don't let it be because you murder, steal, make trouble, or try to control other people's lives" (1 Peter 4:15, ERV).
   Do your friends offer unsolicited advice as a form of control? Are they busybodies? Do your friends have agendas for your life that you never agreed to? Real friends don't try to control you.

Boundaries protect people from unwarranted interference in their lives. We have the right to negotiate who we are and how we want to interact with the world around us. See **Boundaries: What's Okay and Not Okay** at the end of this chapter.

Over-functioning is doing for others what they can and should do for themselves. Usually, over-functioners struggle with people-pleasing. See ***The Rights that People Pleasers Need to Know*** on the next page.

The Rights that People-Pleasers Need to Know

You'll never be loved if you can't risk being disliked.

I put together a list of the rights that people-pleasers need to know about, as they are inclined to let other people govern their lives. Some people-pleasers put other people's needs first as the price of admission to a relationship. If you are a people-pleaser, use this list as a guide as you take the steps to getting your life back from those who didn't know or didn't care to know that you have not been acting from a genuine, self-motivated place but from a fear-based, request-driven place that controls and drives your whole life.

Let's look at what people-pleasers believe they must always do:

1. **Always give**: People-pleasers believe that whenever someone needs, expects, or wants something from them, they must *always* be available to accommodate. What they need to know is that they have the right to evaluate whether their limits of time, money, energy, resources etc. can accommodate the wants, expectations, or needs of others. This requires you to be aware of your resources and limits.

2. **Always agree**: People-pleasers believe that you need to agree with their decisions, and they need to agree with yours, in order for decisions to be valid. What they need to know is that everyone has the right to make decisions and feel confident and happy about those decisions, apart from the agreement of others. They also need to know they have the right to change their minds about a decision upon further consideration. No one needs to offer a rationale or reasons for their behavior, unless the decision affects others.

3. **Always impress**: People-pleasers believe they should never disappoint anyone or fall short of people's invalid expectations of them. See the section on valid expectations below. What they need to know is that they have the right to be imperfect, to make mistakes, and to take responsibility for their mistakes.

4. **Always smile**: People-pleasers believe they always have to be nice, upbeat, and never hurt anyone's feeling. What they need to know is that they have the right to be stern with people and express their emotions

appropriately. Unfortunately, this may hurt some people, but it's important to remember that there's a difference between hurt and harm. Hurt is when pain is inflicted for someone's growth, because the wounds from a friend can be trusted (Proverbs 27:6, NIV). Harm occurs when someone's well-being is damaged.

5. **Always fix things**: People-pleasers believe they must have the answer to every problem in every situation for every person, and they must take care of everyone, whether help is requested or not. What they need to know is that they have the right to determine if they are responsible for finding solutions to everyone's problems. Each of us has the right to ask questions, take the time we need to respond, and say, "I don't know." Or "I don't understand." Or "I can support you in solving this problem, but it's not my problem." Or lastly, "No."

6. **Always do it alone**. People-pleasers believe that they should never ask for help with their needs or problems. What they need to know is that they have the right to ask for what they want and for their needs to be taken seriously.

I hope this list serves you on your journey to getting your life back. Review this list regularly to evaluate your past and current choices to determine if there is a need to pull back and readjust what you're giving. Try to recognize if you are someone who manipulates and uses people-pleasers for your own benefit. Let this be a moment of awakening for you, an awakening that you are robbing someone of their destiny. Each person has their own personal power to direct their life; for whatever reason, people-pleasers give their power away. As a responsible, loving, and moral person, make sure that you are honoring people's decisions and ensuring that they are not being used, but are serving out of a genuine motivation.

Exercise for the People-Pleasers

Practice saying a powerful word, a two-letter word that people-pleasers struggle with. It requires a backbone to say it and mean it. It's the word, "No."

Here are a set of scenarios that can come up over the course of your life that you may have to say "no" to:

1. **Scenario**: A financially irresponsible person who already owes you money asks, "Can I borrow some money? "
   Best answer: "I want to help, but I can't loan you anything until I am confident that you will pay me back."
   Suggestion: I had someone in my life who would ask me for money constantly and never paid me back. I eventually recognized I was enabling bad behavior. I told this person, the next time they asked for money, that I needed to see a budget of their expenses and a time frame to pay it back. I even offered to help them develop a budget. Needless to say, it's been years since this person has asked me for money. This is what happens when you challenge people to be accountable for their decisions instead of enabling them. This lesson is one we all have to learn. Sadly, some people never care to.
2. **Scenario**: You need to study for a test, but your friends invite you to a movie.
   Best answer: "I really want to, but the reality of my school schedule says I can't."
   Note: I remember failing exams because I spent time hanging out when I should have been studying. When I failed, no one was there to help me to cope with the pain. Some people felt sorry for me, but no one was responsible but me. I carry that lesson with me until this day, and I hope you will, too.
3. **Scenario**: Your friends ask you to do something that is against your values and beliefs.
   Best answer: No.
   Note: I remember wrestling with these decisions in my younger days. Social pressure can be difficult at any age. It helped me to remember that each time I did something contrary to my value system, it weakened by character—and that character would be the same one that I would carry with me into every situation for the rest of my life.
4. **Scenario**: You have an important work meeting in thirty minutes, and your always-late friend asks for a quick ride to the airport.
   Best answer: No.
   Note: This might sound cruel, but for all my last-minute people who live in their own time zone, remember that time is the most precious

commodity, because it's irreplaceable. You can't make more and you can't get it back. If you find you are always late to events, please review Chapter 18. As one of my mentors said, you can tell how great of an impact someone will have in life by how they deal with time. I know things happen, but things don't *always* make you late. It's better to learn about the importance of time when the stakes are low, so you won't miss out on a major opportunity when the stakes are higher.

In general, people want to be liked by others, but compromising your deepest values, mental judgment, or emotional safety to please people will only lead to frustration and regrets. *Yes* and *no* are two of the most powerful words in the English language. When you say "no" to something or someone, you have to remember that you're saying "yes" to your values, which affect your schedule. Your schedule affects your rhythm and pace. Your rhythm and pace affect the quality of your life.

A – Agreement and Forgiveness

As I write this, the world is experiencing religious conflicts, ideological reinventions, political confusion, moral vacillation, and social change at a rapid pace. Our situation is laying bare the lack of relational skills that the average person possesses. Because the world has grown more socially complicated, we need to pursue a more nuanced understanding of some social issues.

For the purpose of this section, I will focus on one tool that is necessary, particularly in these times: **Turn to Wonder.**

No two people are the same, so there always will be disagreements. But as two people journey through life together, they need a set of common commitments that allows a friendship to thrive. One of these commitments is an honest, good-faith attempt to understand the other person. See the verses below as a guide to having healthy conversations and debates. In some cases, I have provided two translations that show different nuances.

> **Be humble.** *Live in harmony with one another; do not be haughty [conceited, self-important, exclusive], but associate with humble people [those with a realistic self-view]. Do not overestimate yourself.*
> Romans 12:16, AMP

Agree with one another. Don't be proud. Be willing to be a friend of people who aren't considered important. Don't think that you are better than others.
Romans 12:16, NIRV

Agree in advance to find points of agreement.

Can two people walk together without agreeing on the direction?
Amos 3:3, NLT

Do two people walk hand in hand if they aren't going to the same place?
Amos 3:3, MSG

Don't quarrel with anyone. Be at peace with everyone, just as much as possible.
Romans 12:18, TLB

As much as possible, and to the extent of your ability, live in peace with everyone.
Romans 12:18, NCB

Forgive past mistakes and then let them go.

Whoever forgives someone's sin makes a friend. One who seeks love conceals an offense, but gossiping about the sin [repeating a thing] breaks up friendships.
Proverbs 17:9, EXB

Whoever forgives an offense seeks love, but whoever keeps bringing up the issue separates the closest of friends.
Proverbs 17:9, NOG

Turn to Wonder Reflection Questions[12]

In order to handle each other with care, if you feel judgmental or defensive when someone else is sharing, ask yourself to wonder:

- *What brought her/him to this belief?*
- *What is she/he feeling right now?*
- *What does my reaction teach me about myself?*

T – Trustworthy

> *"Trust" is concerned with the future. It deals with what you will allow yourself to be vulnerable to.*

I want to approach the conversation of trustworthiness on two fronts – character and competence. It's important to work on trustworthiness from the standpoint of proactivity, prevention, and instruction. Remember, trust is lost in buckets and regained in drops.

Character

Character represents a set of attributes that determine your moral and ethical response to circumstances and situations. *Love* is the redemptive, sacrificial, unconditional orientation toward someone's positive well-being. Reflect on the verses and reflection questions below.

> *If you are that kind of person, you can't make up your mind, and you surely can't be trusted. So don't expect the Lord to give you anything at all.*
> James 1:8, CEV

> *An indecisive man is unstable in all his ways.*
> James 1:8, HCSB

> *Do not be so deceived and misled! Evil companionships (communion, associations) corrupt and deprave good manners and morals and character.*
> 1 Cor. 15:33, AMPC

> *Like a muddied fountain and a polluted spring is a righteous man who yields, falls down, and compromises his integrity before the wicked.*
> Proverbs 25:26, AMPC

Reflection and Assessment Questions

1. Are you judgmental and critical of others, or are you someone who provides constructive feedback?
2. Do you gossip about other people, or do you keep the confidences they share?
3. Are you lazy, or do you spend time working on activities that can benefit you and the community?
4. Do you hold on to grudges and find ways to get revenge on others, or do you forgive others and gain wisdom from the experience?
5. Do you have unhealthy habits or addictions that you need to stop? Have you found ways to get help in dealing with your issues, like attending a support group or seeing counselor?
6. When you listen to music, watch movies or shows, or visit websites, do they offer mostly negative content that will not help you to be wiser, more thoughtful, or better as a person?
7. What kind of place would this world be if everybody in it was just like you? What if everyone worked like you or served like you or thought like you or forgave like you? Would the world be better or worse than it is now?
8. Are you a person of your word? Can people count on you to following through on what you say or do?

Competence

In 18,000 police departments, among more than 800,000 sworn law enforcement officers, the conversations happening as I write this are about *de-escalation* – reducing the intensity of potentially violent situations or conflicts. This emphasis is a response to infamous occasions when routine or casual interactions between law enforcement and unarmed people of color ended with the loss of life. This conversation is one that will be ongoing. The topic requires a depth of knowledge and critical thinking, and a high degree of maturity.

On a more personal level, we can learn how to keep bad things from happening in our friendships. How do you keep small things from becoming big things? Relational struggles don't typically get better with time. They get better with knowledge and intentional application of that knowledge over a consistent period of time.

Below are the exercises listed in Part 1. Cultivate these skills until they become automatic. You will get out of the process what you put into it.

1) Expressing appreciations and sharing new Information – Chapter 1
2) Clearing up assumptions and setting valid expectations – Chapter 2
3) Understanding your family background and what cycles need to be broken – Chapter 3
4) Listening without an agenda – Chapter 4
5) Speaking your values in a safe space – Chapter 5
6) Fighting cleanly – Chapter 6

Boundaries: What's Okay and Not Okay

Givers have to set limits, because takers never do.

Boundaries are the informal rules that tell us what's acceptable and not acceptable in a relationship. Boundaries protect things that are valuable to us. In a perfect world, we would be able to pursue our goals and dreams for our life without any issues. Everyone would support us wholeheartedly and considerately. No one would disagree with our beliefs, values, or vision.

Sadly, that's not how this world works. We continually have to raise the issue of boundaries and learn how to apply them in a healthy way. Boundaries ensure that we are not living anyone else's life. They protect what is most precious to us, which allows us to love well.

Over the years, I have heard countless stories of people who have been so emotionally, psychologically, or physically wounded that their lives became full of fear. They were controlled by the thoughts and opinions of others. These stories all include poor boundaries, a poor sense of self, and a lack of healthy self-regard. Like many of us, these individuals never learned the necessity of the ability to set boundaries. Just like dominoes, the moment one boundary falls, the rest coming crashing down. These people are routinely victims of damaging relationships.

It's never too late to learn to set and defend your boundaries. I would like to highlight four areas where it is extremely important to establish boundaries—time, talents, treasures, and thoughts—and also provide practical instructions for how it can be done.

Time

The one commodity that cannot be replaced is time. I have a friend who says, "If you waste my money, I can make more. If you waste my food, I can buy more. But if you waste my time, I can never get that back." I've learned to take this very seriously over the years, because of the potential devastating consequences. Boundaries around time are important, because time is a finite resource. You only get so many hours in a day and you can use that time toward something productive or lose it by not deciding at all.

Here are several tips that can be used in protecting and planning your time:

-Identify your MIT (Most Important Task) and do it first
-Work from your calendar, not a to-do list,
-Overcome procrastination by thinking of your future self
-Always carry a notebook to record helpful insights and reminders
-Control your inbox and text messages use
-Schedule and attend meetings as a last resort
-Say no to everything that doesn't support your immediate goals
-If you can do a task in less than five minutes, do it immediately

See Chapter 18 of **Bridge the Gaps** for a helpful tool in naming and managing your priorities well, so you can use your time wisely.

Talents

A talent is defined as a naturally recurring pattern of thought, feeling, or behavior that can be used in a fruitful way. Talents are given to everyone, but strength is given to those who work for it. You develop strengths by working on your craft over time. It's important to practice persistently and consistently so you can stay within striking distance of excellence. This takes work.

The important thing to remember is that you are responsible for the naming, cultivation, and use of your gifts and talents. Here's a question that motivates me: If you have the ability to better, then why aren't you? The benefits of working on your skills and talents are worth it. As the Scripture says, observe people who are good at their work. Skilled workers are always in demand and admired; they don't take a backseat to anyone. (Proverbs 22:29, MSG).

I see so many people who spend their lives living out someone else's script. They waste their time by investing in the wrong things or people, and they neglect to improve themselves. Boundaries help you to continue to love what you do and were made to do and avoid taking on things you shouldn't. Boundaries remind us that there is a destination.

You have to remember the one thing you can never do in life: *pleasing everyone*. This is the biggest trap that people fall into, especially the "nice" people, which is really code for people-pleaser. One speaker said, "I don't know how to be successful, but I do know how to fail. Try to please everyone."

Your life matters, and anyone who truly cares for you will want you to make the most of it by taking the time to improve your skills and abilities. See Chapter 4 on finding your talents and Chapter 24 on using the 10,000-hour rule to achieve mastery of your gifts and talents.

Treasures

Your treasures represent your money. There's not a topic in my life where I have seen more conflict. Whether it's not having enough, having enough but mismanaging it, lending or borrowing money, or having too much and losing sight of priorities, money affects almost every dimension of life.

Boundaries are important with money because it is a resource to help you move through life with options. Chapter 14 is the chapter on money. Please review this lesson, which provides simple principles and tools in how to think about and manage your money.

I want to deal with the topic of borrowing and lending money. As the Scripture says, just as the rich rule the poor, so the borrower is servant to the lender (Proverbs 22:7, NLT). This is an extreme picture of the relationship that money creates when that money is borrowed and lent.

Lending

As a rule, I personally do not let people borrow money unless I'm ready to lose it. Over time, I have seen numerous examples of relationships in families and friendships destroyed because of unpaid loans and unhealthy ways of dealing with the default of the loans. When loans are not repaid, it causes resentment, slander, factions over who's right and wrong, and a whole host of other issues. When it comes to lending money, it really doesn't become a problem until you don't have enough.

I recommend that if someone is asking you to borrow money and you do not have your emergency fund in place (as discussed in Chapter 14), it would be wise to decline to help. But the circumstances of a situation can be complicated, and it's tougher when the borrower is closer to home.

Take time to assess several things. This is not an exhaustive list, but all these things are important for your consideration:

Things to consider:

- **The financial responsibility** of the person asking for money. Are they dependable and reliable when it comes to paying their debts?
- **The circumstances** of the loan. Is the person borrowing money because they want to go on vacation or because they need to pay for their rent or face eviction?
- **Your current financial condition**. Are you in a position to help someone financially? Are you struggling financially? Do you have your three to six months of emergency expenses in place?

Use these questions in evaluating whether you should let someone borrow your money. It's often less complicated to just give the person whatever you can comfortably afford, as a gift.

Borrowing

Have you been in the position of having to borrow money from others to get through a tough situation? I recommend you try not to make a habit of it. If you do borrow money, do everything within your power and honor to return the funds in the time promised. Don't make the lender ask for repayment.

As a precaution, do everything to put yourself on a good financial footing through strong financial disciplines such as budgeting, living below your means, and financial goal-setting. These are discussed in Chapter 14.

Thoughts

When I was in high school, I heard a really good piece of advice from a motivational speaker that has stuck with me. He said, "If you don't know what you believe about a particular topic, read two books on it and then make up your own mind." The essence of the message was: Be sure that what you do is a product of your own conclusions. We need to own our beliefs and attitudes, because they fall within our property line. As the Scripture teaches, the gullible believe anything they are told, but the prudent sift and weigh every word (Proverbs 14:15, MSG).

Three things that you should do:

1. **Evaluate**: Take the time to evaluate the beliefs and philosophies you have. It's okay to say, "I don't know right now. Let me think about it." One of the worst things that I see happen is people rushing to a conclusion about serious life matters due to outside pressure. Chapter 7 is a tool that you can use for this practice.
2. **Keep growing**: Continue to expand your mind by taking in new information. You will be transformed by the renewing of your mind. See Chapter 16 of **Bridge the Gaps** for more on personal development.
3. **Get help**: Sometimes we all have what my counselor friend calls "stinking thinking." This is a type of thinking that is distorted, unhealthy and can lead to decisions that are bad for your life. Bad thinking might be black and white thinking, emotional reasoning, jumping to conclusions, minimizing, overgeneralizing, and more. I recommend sitting with a certified coach or licensed counselor to discuss the tools and how to apply them to sort out what you truly believe.

– 13 –

Dreams to Reality: Get a Vision or Perish

Dreams will remain dreams unless they generate a clear vision of what you want to happen.

The outgrowth of your purpose will be dreams, visions, and goals. At the heart of a dream is the change that you want to see. A dream is a cherished aspiration, ambition, or ideal. Our dreams and visions push us forward, mandate our focus, spark creativity, and stir a sense of urgency and toughness. They keep us motivated and persistent.

One of the ways to turn dreams into reality is to get information and reflect on it. You will bring to fruition what you have the most clarity on. That's why education is so vital. You want to relentlessly search for models and systems that can help you get where you want to go and accomplish the purpose you have in mind.

"Hope that is put off makes the heart sick, but a desire that comes into being is a tree of life" (Proverbs 13:12, NLV). Real pleasure comes from seeing what you envision in your mind become reality. It all starts with the dream.

Human beings, through our remarkable sense of imagination, have the ability to finish something before we start it. Everything you see in the manmade world began as a thought in someone's mind. You can, in your own way, become a resident of a world that does not yet exist. When you experience the realization of your vision, you'll feel a joy like no other, particularly if you put in the hours, days, months, and even years to reach that goal.

When I reached major goals in my life, I realized how people feel when they win championships, pass difficult tests, and get accepted into their schools of choice.

Bryan Stevenson, the author of *Just Mercy, A Story of Justice and Redemption*, is the founder of Equal Justice Initiative (www.eji.org), a human rights organization in Montgomery, Alabama. Through his work as a public interest lawyer for the incarcerated, the condemned, and the poor, he has saved dozens of innocent people from the death penalty.

In short, Stevenson's work is a miracle, because he didn't meet a lawyer until he got to law school. By his tenacity and God's grace, he stuck to his ideals and tried to become something he'd never seen.

When he got to Harvard's law school, he was tempted to compromise and settle for a life that he was not meant to live. In school, he didn't hear anything that addressed race, poverty, and inequality—the topics he cared most about. But he refused to become well-adjusted to injustice and pursue the corrupted American Dream of peacocking and posturing.

His dream went further. He had a dream of justice. Believing the dots would connect, he followed his convictions, though they led him off the well-worn path. I believe that God gives us lamps so that we can take the next step, even when we can't see the road ahead.

We are all capable of having big ideas about what life is and should be like. Unfortunately, many of us were not given the space to express our unique ambitions. Lerone Bennett, Jr., a black scholar and social historian, was a student at Morehouse College in 1945 with Dr. Martin Luther King, Jr. He admits that he knew King would go on to do something great, but he didn't know that Dr. King would turn the world upside-down.

The moral that Bennett drew is that, because of the mystery of the human personality, there is no way to tell what someone might accomplish. When we plan the course of our lives, we must give ourselves permission to operate within the context of the dreams we have.

You want to ground your dreams in reality and then set out in a positive direction to find out if the dream is a possibility or just a fantasy. Grounding is part of the goal-setting process.

As Proverbs 28:19 (NIV) says: "Those who work their land will have abundant food, but those who chase fantasies will have their fill of poverty." A *dream* is rooted in reality and backed by work (such as building a career). A *fantasy* is rooted in fiction and laziness (such as winning the lottery).

When you focus on what's possible instead of what's difficult, your dream becomes attainable. You see the opportunity instead of the obligation. Bryan Stevenson's dream was justice and social equality. He was willing to wake up early, stay up late, and allow his life to be animated by this dream. Each day he worked toward his dream of justice for the most underserved people in society.

Here are some exercises to help you turn your dream into reality:

Exercise #1: Name Your Dream

After completing the first section and writing your purpose statement, you now want to begin to identify what dream (cherished aspiration, ambition, or ideal) moves you in this season of your life.

_____

_____

_____

_____

_____

_____

_____

_____

_____

_____

_____

Exercise #2: Write Your Vision

> *And then God answered: "Write this. Write what you see. Write it out in big block letters so that it can be read on the run. This vision-message is a witness pointing to what's coming. It aches for the coming—it can hardly wait! And it doesn't lie. If it seems slow in coming, wait. It's on its way. It will come right on time."*
> Habakkuk 2:2, MSG

The greatest pull on your life should be the pull of your dream. Your life is unique, so the manifestation of your dream must be unique as well. Once that dream is well-designed, you can face the future with anticipation instead of apprehension. When the future gets clear, the price seems easier.

If you have identified a dream, keep searching for it. My hope is that the uniqueness of your purpose will transform into practical, time-stamped goals. Acknowledging and celebrating the past is great, but without a vision of how to improve on the past, we will never move forward.

The first thing you want to bring into focus is your mental picture of your goal fulfilled. That's where the improvement begins, because you can only hit what you aim at. Writing down your goals speaks to your belief that it is worth taking the time to give your life structure. With each action you take, you're painting the picture of the vision you possess.

It's been said that we overrate what we can do in a year and underrate what we can do in ten years, so let your goals reflect long-term as well as short-term visions. What plans do you have for the next six months, one year, three years, or five years to bring your dream to life?

Six-month goal(s)/plan(s)

_____

_____

One-year goal(s)/plan(s)

_____

_____

Three-year goal(s)/plan(s)

_____

_____

Five-year goal(s)/plan(s)

_____

_____

Ten-year goal(s)/plan(s)

_____

_____

Exercise 3: Execute on Your Plan: The Visible Made by the Invisible

A well-thought-out plan will work to your advantage,
but hasty actions will cost you dearly.
Proverbs 21:5, VOICE

The legendary football coach Tony Dungy said that many people do things in life, finances, and family matters that they would never do on the football field: being unprepared, undisciplined, and unfocused.

Planning is bringing the future into the present so you can do something about it now. Many people drift and allow the circumstances of life to dictate their plans and goals. You need to have your own self-direction, self-enterprise, self-reliance, and self-discipline. When you plan, you are deciding and arranging things in advance. To do that, you will need abstract tools like perseverance, discipline, and creativity.

Below is a list of the tools needed to create and execute on a plan. I refer to them as Productivity Tools. Chapter references are from ***Bridge the Gaps – Lessons on Self-Awareness, Self-Development, and Self-Care:***

1. **Set Your Goals** – When something is important enough, the odds don't matter. Get proximate to the places that will animate your purpose and allow your dream to develop its own footing. While in law school, Bryan Stevenson eagerly signed up for a class on poverty and race litigation that required him to work at a social justice organization. Through this experience, he met a black man on death row who was the same age he was. This led him to fight harder to learn the laws and doctrines that shape policy and criminal procedure. (Chapter 11)
2. **Define Your Success** – One of our greatest fears should be succeeding at things that don't matter. As you develop a plan for each dimension of life, don't waste your time and energy. (Chapter 12)
3. **Develop Your Self-Regard** – Learn to have confidence in yourself and your skills, because a man without confidence loses twice. (Chapter 13)
4. **Get Control of Your Finances** – Money does not come with instructions. You must determine a structure for your financial life. (Chapter 14)

5. **Learn about SMART Goals** – In order to do what's impossible, you have to start with what's possible. Create goals that are specific, measurable, authored, relevant, and time-based. (Chapter 15)
6. **Work on Personal Development** – How far you go might be determined by what you're exposed to. Create a list of books to read in your area of choice. Stevenson made a list of the classes he would take to educate himself about the death penalty and extreme punishments. Most people who don't succeed in what they are going after have not taken the time to research. People often ask for things and then see if they want them. You can anticipate and save precious time if you do your research first. (Chapter 16)
7. **Decide Where You'll Put Your Time and Focus** – Much of your progress will be a direct reflection of the work that you put in. Decide now to place premium value on the way you spend your time. (Chapter 18 and 19)
8. **Work on Your Self-Discipline** – Are you able to carry out plans after the thrill of a new project has passed? Perseverance gets many things accomplished that creativity cannot. (Chapter 21)
9. **Perfect Your Environment** – You want to be around people, places, and things that allow you to stumble, crawl, and walk to your greatness and also motivate you to be better. Recognize that you are vulnerable to the input of those around you. Identify whom you can connect with and learn from to help you realize your dream. It's difficult to accomplish a goal when you're not accustomed to seeing other people accomplish anything. If you can become successful, you can set the example. (Chapter 22)
10. **Learn How to Make Decisions** – Find credible information sources. The worst advisors and least credible sources of information that I hear referenced are "they said" and "I heard." Do your homework before you decide. (Chapter 23)
11. **Be Willing to Put in the 10,000 Hours** – Know that it might take 10,000 hours to become skillful enough to accomplish your goal. Make it a goal to master whatever craft will serve your purpose. *"If you are uniquely gifted in your work, you will rise and be promoted. You won't be held back— you'll stand before kings"* (Proverbs 22:29, TPT). (Chapter 24)

12. **Develop Habits and Systems** – Create a routine to support your purpose. Re-evaluate and revise your habits whenever necessary to keep steering yourself toward your goal. (Chapter 25)
13. **Learn About Problem-Solving** – Problems are an opportunity to put your best and most creative effort forward. Instead of being discouraged, see problems as an opportunity to hone your problem-solving skills. (Chapter 26)
14. **Face Your Obstacles** – As a man, you need to be able to control your emotions and avoid losing your head when things get tough. There will be obstacles, but you'll also find ways to climb over them. (Chapter 27)
15. **Learn to Accept Setbacks** – Failures are part of the road to success. Many people who want to accomplish things have no idea what it's going to cost them. The price of success is often a series of temporary setbacks. Every dream takes longer than you want it to. (Chapter 28)
16. **Overcome Your Fear of Success** – The worst kind of sabotage is self-sabotage. You need the right mentality as you move to new levels of expectation and the confidence to know you'll be able to handle achievement. (Chapter 29)
17. **Embrace Change** – How you deal with change and stress determines how fast you level up or if you manage to transition at all. (Chapter 30)

A more detailed discussion of these skills can be found in ***Bridge the Gaps – Lessons on Self-Awareness, Self-Development, and Self-Care.*** Go to **www.thebridge330.com** to pick up a copy.

Encouragement/Reminders When Times Get Tough

1. Jesus was resolute in the face of possible danger. Be like Jesus.
   At that time some Pharisees came to Jesus and said to him, "Leave this place and go somewhere else. Herod wants to kill you." He replied, "Go tell that fox, 'I will keep on driving out demons and healing people today and tomorrow, and on the third day I will reach my goal.' (Luke 13:31-32, NIV)
2. Jesus set boundaries around his purpose and plan. Be like Jesus
   At daybreak, Jesus went out to a solitary place. The people were looking for him and when they came to where he was, they tried to keep him from leaving them. But he said, "I must proclaim the good news of the kingdom of God to the other towns also, because that is why I was sent." (Luke 4:42-43, NIV)
3. It's good for us to experience pressure to reach goals, so that when life gets really challenging, we can handle the pressure.
   Don't run from tests and hardships, brothers and sisters. As difficult as they are, you will ultimately find joy in them; if you embrace them, your faith will blossom under pressure and teach you true patience as you endure. And true patience brought on by endurance will equip you to complete the long journey and cross the finish line—mature, complete, and wanting nothing. (James 1:2-4, The Voice)
4. Do everything you have been instructed to do, and trust God with the rest.
   Only be strong and very courageous, that you may observe to do according to all the law which Moses my servant commanded you; do not turn from it to the right hand or to the left, that you may prosper wherever you go. This Book of the Law shall not depart from your mouth, but you shall meditate in it day and night, that you may observe to do according to all that is written in it. For then you will make your way prosperous, and then you will have good success. Have I not commanded you? Be strong and of good courage; do not be afraid, nor be dismayed, for the Lord your God is with you wherever you go. (Joshua 1:7-9, NKJV)

− 14 −

Develop a Code of Conduct: Log Out and Check Yourself So No One Has To

Whoever obeys a commandment keeps himself safe, but someone who is contemptuous in conduct will die.
Proverbs 19:16, ISV

We have to learn to love ourselves and each other enough to have principles, boundaries, and expectations govern our behavior, because that will ensure we can sustainably fight the forces that would attempt to undermine our effectiveness.

As the Word says, "First take the log out of your own eye, and then you will be able to see clearly to take the speck out of your brother's eye" (Matthew 7:5, GNT).

As I think of ruined legacies of high-profile people (too many to name), I can't help but think of how these individuals could have gone down in history as successful men who lived great and impactful lives. Unfortunately, their legacies are permanently marred because of unethical things they did behind the scenes, leaving behind emotional wreckage and many unanswered questions.

One of the main, painstaking lessons that I've learned is that the greatest threat to freedom *is* your freedom. You want to use your freedom to make the right and best things happen and to keep the wrong things from happening.

Many people were never taught to have consequential thinking. They didn't consider the possible consequences of their actions, which is a type of thinking they should have learned in adolescence.

Part of being confident comes from knowing that you have to put the controls in place in your life to keep negative things from happening. It involves choosing your future by how you act in the present. For that, you need a code of conduct.

A code of conduct is a set of moral principles, boundaries, and expectations that are incorporated into your life, which keep you from sabotaging, interrupting, or detouring your life's purpose.

A code of conduct provides guidance to avoid temptations and prevent pitfalls—taking proactive steps instead of focusing on a cure after the damage is done. If you are not given a code, you'll never learn—or worse, you'll learn from the wrong places. I know from experience that the pain of regret is heavier than the pain of proactivity.

No one talks about the foundation of a house until the house is falling apart—yet the foundation is the hardest and most important part of building a house. Your code of conduct is the foundation to your life.

When you define the way you plan to conduct yourself, publicly and privately, you give yourself the best chance to build and improve your character, your confidence, and subsequently, your destiny.

What might be some of the negative things you want to keep from happening? Let me give you a list. These are the consequences of having no code of conduct.

Poor eating/sleep/exercise habits lead to:
Preventable diseases, low energy, poor mental/emotional/physical health

Poor self-control/due diligence concerning your financial life leads to:
Unmanageable debts, relational conflict due to financial stress, foreclosures, property repossessions, legal problems

Poor sexual/relational practices can lead to:
STDs, unwanted pregnancies, child-support battles, lifelong relational drama

Poor relationship choices lead to:
Long-term relational turmoil, community breakdown, and misguided choices, including breaking the law

Poor emotional habits lead to:
Using addictions to cope with your emotional pain, impulsive actions

Poor time management results in:
Missed deadlines and opportunities, leading to life-altering circumstances

What if you made mistakes because you never had a code of conduct to guide your behavior and choices? Then you must *forgive yourself* and learn the lessons. My faith tradition teaches me that God can *restore to you the years that the swarming locust has eaten.* (Joel 2:25, NKJV.) The second half of your life can be better than the first half, especially if you have learned the lessons of the first half.

Sample Code of Conduct

Here's a sample code of conduct with examples of specific actions that this person decides to incorporate:

1. **Mental/Personal Development:** I will read two books a month based on my personal and professional developmental needs.
2. **Social/Professional:** I will arrive everywhere I am scheduled to go on time and adequately prepared for my responsibilities.
3. **Community-Building Habit:** I will offer my seat to anyone who needs it more than I do if limited seating is available.
4. **Financial:** I will meet with my financial advisor quarterly.
5. **Financial:** I will budget my money properly every week to live below my means.
6. **Financial/Relational:** I will not loan money to others unless I am prepared to not have it paid back.
7. **Relational:** I will settle serious interpersonal conflict privately, personally, and peacefully.
8. **Physical:** I will commit to eating healthy food (high-fiber, low-sodium) and working out at least four times a week.
9. **Spiritual/Relational:** I will refuse to gossip, slander, or speak of someone in a negative way.
10. **Relational**: I will keep my commitments and refrain from committing in a way that exceeds my limits.
11. **Spiritual:** I will see a spiritual counselor once a month or more. This serves as a spiritual checkup to exercise spiritual disciplines. (James 5:16, NIV)
12. **Spiritual:** I will preserve the preciousness of sexual intimacy within the context of marriage.
13. **Spiritual:** I won't use social media more than once a month.
14. **Spiritual:** I won't watch shows with sexually explicit content.
15. **Spiritual/Relational:** I will break contact with all relationships that don't contribute to my overall well-being and purpose.

Personal Code of Conduct

Take some time to come up with your own code of conduct based on who you want to be and the kind of man you want to become. This is personal, so consider your personal history. Identify areas where your history indicates you might need improvement.

1. _____
2. _____
3. _____
4. _____
5. _____
6. _____
7. _____
8. _____

For additional exercises and tools, see Chapter 25 – Habits and Systems in ***Bridge the Gaps: Lessons on Self-Awareness, Self-Development and Self-Care***. Visit www.barnesandnoble.com, www.amazon.com or **www.thebridg330.com** to pick up a copy.

Bridge the Gaps Code of Conduct

Here's my code of conduct based on the guide *Bridge the Gaps – Lessons on Self-Awareness, Self-Development, and Self-Care*.

1. **I will choose my environment and friends wisely.**
    a. *Do not be misled: Bad company corrupts good character.* (1 Corinthians 15:33, NLT)
    b. *The righteous choose their friends carefully, but the way of the wicked leads them astray.* (Proverbs 12:26, KJV)
    c. Read Chapters 22 and 33 of ***Bridge the Gaps***.
2. **I will deal with temptations graciously and firmly.**
    a. *Dear brothers and sisters, is your life full of difficulties and temptations? Then be happy, for when the way is rough, your patience has a chance to grow. So let it grow, and don't try to squirm out of your problems. For when your patience is finally in full bloom, then you will be ready for anything, strong in character, full and complete.* (James 1:2-4, TLB)
    b. Read Chapters 26, 27, 28, and 30 of ***Bridge the Gaps***.

3. **I won't venture past my sphere of knowledge until my sphere of knowledge exceeds my venture.**
    a. *Desire without knowledge is not good — how much more will hasty feet miss the way!* (Proverbs 19:2, NIV)
    b. Read Chapters 7, 9, and 16 of ***Bridge the Gaps***.

4. **I will work to achieve mastery of myself and my craft.**
    a. *Do you see someone skilled in their work? They will serve before kings; they will not serve before officials of low rank.* (Proverbs 22:29, NIV)
    b. Read Chapters 4, 6, and 24 of ***Bridge the Gaps***.

5. **I will cultivate a vision and work hard to bring it into fruition.**
    a. *All hard work brings a profit, but mere talk leads only to poverty.* (Proverbs 14:23, NIV)
    b. *Where there is no vision, the people perish.* (Proverbs 29:18, KJV)
    c. Read Chapters 8 and 20 of ***Bridge the Gaps***.

6. **I will make fewer announcements and more adjustments.**
   a. *Like billowing clouds that bring no rain is the person who talks big but never produces.* (Proverbs 25:14, MSG)
   b. Read Chapter 15 of ***Bridge the Gaps.***

7. **I will eliminate distractions and identify my focus.**
   a. *No one serving as a soldier gets entangled in civilian affairs, but rather tries to please his commanding officer.* (2 Timothy 2:4, NIV)
   b. Read Chapters 1, 12, 17, and 29 of ***Bridge the Gaps.***

8. **I'll remember that I don't have to be great to get started, but I have to get started to be great.**
   a. *Do not despise these small beginnings.* (Zechariah 4:10, NLT)
   b. Read Chapter 11 of ***Bridge the Gaps.***

9. **I will manage my priorities wisely.**
   a. *Teach us to number our days, that we may gain a heart of wisdom.* (Psalm 90:12, NIV)
   b. Read Chapters 18, 19, 23, and 43 of ***Bridge the Gaps.***

10. **I will learn to love myself and others.**
    a. *Let your love abound in knowledge and depth of insight.* (Philippians 1:9, NIV)
    b. Read Chapters 31 to 42 of ***Bridge the Gaps.***

15

Sweat Equity: Put in the Work to Become an Emotionally Mature (Loving) Adult

If you're reading this and you're from a family that has not embodied the culture of love that this book talks about—and you want to break cycles—this message is for you.

It's been said that children don't do well at obeying their parents, but they have no problem imitating them. Unfortunately, for many of the young people I work with, their first observation of their families teaches them unhealthy ways of coping. In fact, most of their families remain in a persistent state of breakdown over unresolved issues and unmet expectations.

Each generation has a responsibility to be more ethical and resourceful than the generation that came before it. I think this presents a great opportunity for young people to follow this biblical injunction:

> *And don't be intimidated by those who are older than you; simply be the example they need to see by being faithful and true in all that you do. Speak the truth and live a life of purity and **authentic love** as you remain strong in your faith.*
> 1 Timothy 4:12, TPT

> *Don't let anyone look down on you because you are young. Set an example for the believers in what you say and in how you live. Also set an example in **how you love** and in what you believe. Show the believers how to be pure.*
> 1 Timothy 4:12, NIRV

Change is about interrupting patterns that no longer serve you. Changing the way we love will not come by fighting the old. It will come by building the new.

Abuse and violence can destroy a relationship, family, or community. Neglect can, too, including

- Neglect expressing appreciation for others

- Neglect sharing your life in healthy ways with others
- Neglect honoring one another's differences
- Neglecting to resolve conflicts in a healthy way
- Neglect protecting your boundaries and the boundaries of others.

If you continue to neglect, it's safe to say that, in time, the relationship, family, community will destroy itself.

That's why Jesus called Satan a thief (John 10:10). By stealing the desire and/or the ability to love, he leaves us in a condition of chronic relationship breakdown. He knows that, without love, the best parts of mankind will be destroyed.

Let's not be arrogant about our ability to love. There's no silver bullet when it comes to learning how to love. We can only practice and incorporate these skills on a consistent basis until they become part of the culture, prioritized and owned by each individual and each community. These are not skills that I have mastered. They are skills that I never learned in my youth, and because of that, I experienced relational turmoil as an adult. Sadly, I know I am not alone.

It's important to note that by no means are the tools in this book comprehensive. I simply captured that tools that I believe the greatest number of people will need in their toolbox in light of the social, cultural climate that exists in the time of writing this book.

The process of building a healthy life and healthy relationships will include starts, stops, delays, detours, confusion, and seasons of being lost—only to find your way again, if you stay on the road. It's not about intensity. It's about consistency. The most valuable commodity is time. Because procrastination is the thief of time and teaches you that you don't have to pay for something now, it will serve us well to begin immediately applying these skills to relationships, so that we can get on the road to building better communities and we don't have to pay later.

The skills, practices, and tools of loving well take time to cultivate and implement. It's almost like working muscles in your body you've never used. As you put the work in, you'll begin to experience emotions and thoughts that might feel strange. Be patient with yourself and others if you begin this journey.

We live in a world that focuses on being effective, often in the short term, and then loses sight of being faithful to ethical standards of care for our fellow man. As one leader says, we love things and use people, instead of using things and loving people. My hope is that this guide will serve as a catalyst for a shift in our definitions of success, so that we will be inclusive of others and love others well.

I want to see a better world. My hope is that this work can spark minds and motivate people to take action to be emotionally healthy and mature. Then we can heal hearts that can change the world.

Choosing a Counselor[13]

In choosing a counselor, always keep in mind that you are a consumer. You are purchasing a service from a professional and have choices about whether you want to begin such a relationship. These are some questions you might ask:

1. What are your techniques of training, experience, and specialization?
2. Are there particular techniques you use?
3. Will you discuss my treatment plan with me?
4. What happens if we disagree about my goals?
5. Are you licensed by or registered with the state?
6. Have you ever had a charge of unethical conduct brought against you?
7. For what length of time do you usually treat clients?
8. Is there anyone with whom you will be discussing my case?
9. Have you had experience with other people in similar situations?
10. Do you charge for an initial consultation?
11. Do you charge for a telephone consultation?
12. How much do you charge for each counseling session?
13. Will my insurance pay for this counseling?
14. How long will our appointments be?
15. If I decide that I would like to work with you, are there any other interviews that you require me to complete?

Many therapists gain clients through word of mouth, and certainly hearing good things about a therapist is a promising sign that the therapist that was good for your friend might also be good for you. But just as you won't necessarily like all your friend's friends, you won't necessarily "click" with your friend's choice of therapist.

You need to like and respect your therapist or you will not be open to what they say to you. You should also feel comfortable enough with your therapist that you could say anything to them and you would not feel that they would judge you or think less of you. This is very important, since there may be things that you tell a therapist that you will never tell another person. So it is very important to feel that you trust them and you trust their judgment.

After deciding on a therapist, it is a good idea to give a therapist at least two sessions before you make up your mind about whether you can work with them. If you still feel uncomfortable, it might be time to find another one. You should also be prepared to feel nervous and uncomfortable at times with your therapist. After all, they are not meant to be a friend who will nod and agree with everything you say. Sometimes therapists can make you feel very uncomfortable indeed, as they slowly move you toward areas in your life that are blocking you that you haven't wanted to deal with. This is where it is important that you have that initial liking and trusting relationship. When things start to get hard in therapy, you need to feel reassured that your therapist is there trying to make your life better and is ultimately on your side.

Occasionally, you will get angry with your therapist, and a good therapist will be able to cope with that and not get angry back at you. An angry therapist is not a good sign, and although rare lapses are acceptable, since we are all human, a therapist who routinely displays frustration at your slow progress or inability to move past a certain difficulty in your life, is not the right therapist for you.

The best relationship is where you are able to look back and see that during the difficult times in your life journey, your therapist was there, like a patient parent, listening, hoping for, and observing your recovery. When you finally get to a resolution, they are almost as pleased as you are!

Resources

If you, or someone you know, is in crisis, please seek help immediately. Contact the following organizations for information about twenty-four-hour crisis services in your area:

The National Suicide Prevention Lifeline's twenty-four-hour, toll-free crisis hotline, 1.800.273.TALK (1.800.273.8255) can put you into contact with your local crisis center, which can tell you where to seek immediate help in your area.

The SAMHSA Substance Abuse Treatment Facility Locator and the SAMHSA 24/7 Treatment and Referral line at 1.800.662.4357 provide referrals to alcohol, substance abuse, and dual-diagnosis treatment facilities, including facilities that offer sliding scale fees and other special payment arrangements. Dual diagnosis services provide integrated treatment for individuals who have both an alcohol or substance abuse problem and a mental illness. They will help you find the facilities that most closely match your needs.

The Child-Help USA 1.800.4.A.CHILD (1.800.422.4453) crisis line assists both child and adult survivors of abuse, including sexual abuse. The hotline, staffed by mental health professionals, also provides treatment referrals.

To locate therapists, you can go to this link http://www.mentalhealthamerica.net/finding-therapy or www.mentalhealth.gov for referrals.

Do everything you can to seek help. Please don't hesitate to contact a trained and licensed counselor for assistance. Whatever you're going through, you don't have to do it alone.

What Is TheBridge330?

TheBridge330 mentoring program was started to provide individuals with the tools to be self-reflective, productive in their purpose, and attentive to their well-being. The values that undergird the program and its mission focus on social change, restoring hope in vulnerable communities, and paving a pathway to emotional health. The name TheBridge330 was chosen for two reasons:

1) TheBridge – As I served in my community over a period of years, there were grassroot realities that consistently emerged, issues like incarceration, recidivism, illiteracy, the long-term effects of child abuse, and fatherlessness. For a bridge to be built for passage over obstacles, the two primary obstacles that need to be addressed are hatred and ignorance, within and without the community. The program is designed to raise awareness of these issues and bring resources to bear.

2) John 3:30 (CEV) says, "Jesus must become more important, while I become less important."
   I learned this passage from the Bible in church as a teenager. In essence, it talks about living like Jesus. As I studied his teachings, several of them emerged as cornerstone philosophies for real healing and social change:

-Take care of the "least of these" (the hungry, thirsty, the stranger, the naked, sick, the imprisoned). (Matthew 25)
-Be like the Good Samaritan who cares for the vulnerable and abandoned. (Luke 10)
-Defend those attacked by unjust and merciless accusers. Then provide the guidance and counsel to help the accused live a life of purpose and turn from the sinful path. (John 8)

-Meet the needs of those without guidance—the sheep without a shepherd. (Mark 6:34)
-Overturn the tables; disrupt the practices of the unscrupulous businesspeople who extort the poor. (John 2:15)

I realized that the example of Jesus is what can truly change our world. That was contrary to what I was living and seeing around me. So I chose to live it out. I've had some tough days and made my fair share of mistakes. At the same time, I was privileged to have the safety and resources needed to find my way to my purpose. Jesus says, "To whom much is given, from him much will be required" (Luke 12:48, NKJV). I chose to teach through writing. To find out more about my mission, check out the following books:

Bridge the Gaps – Lessons on Self-Awareness, Self-Development and Self-Care (Reference: BTG)
-A life coaching framework that provides tools to cultivate a heightened sense of identity and purpose, a growth mindset, and a greater level of emotional health.

The Bridge to Change – Mentoring Tools for Parents, Teachers, Coaches, and Counselors (Reference: TBTC)
-A mentoring guide that provides tools for ending unproductive beliefs, behaviors, and attitudes, while healing the multigenerational transmission of trauma, and leveraging the resilience of people to build a healthier culture.

You can find these books at https://www.barnesandnoble.com, https://www.amazon.com or www.thebridg330.store.

About the Author

Jonathan Frejuste is the creator of TheBridege330, a program whose mission is to provide quality mentoring tools and resources to underserved, under-resourced, and vulnerable communities in ways that support sustained social change, a restoration of hope, and an avenue to emotional health. He is also an Associate Coach with The Center for Emotional Development. He is certified in the emotional measures EQi and EQ 360. He has coached leaders ranging from directors of law enforcement agencies to senior spiritual leaders. He worked as an auditor with Deloitte and Touche, where he earned his CPA (certified public accountant) license and serves as a senior financial planner with Ernst and Young, where he earned his Series 65 Registered Investment Advisor License. He served as a life skills coach at the Somerset Home for Temporarily Displaced Children and was certified as a behavioral assistant with the state of New Jersey's Children's System of Care. He serves schools and non-profits as a speaker, workshop facilitator, and a coach, using the skills he's acquired through his diverse background to provide people with tools and resources to promote and support individual and community well-being.

IG & Twitter: @tb330_mentoring
Website: www.thebridge330.com
E-mail: jon@thebridge330.com

End notes

1. Scazzero, Pete and Geri. *Emotionally Healthy Skills 2.0: Discipleship that Deeply Changes Your Relationship with Others.* Zondervan, 2017 Used with Permission
2. Ibid
3. Ibid
4. Ibid
5. Ibid
6. Ibid
7. Ibid
8. Ibid
9. Ibid
10. Ibid
11. Ibid
12. Ibid
13. Mchugh, Beth "Finding a Good Therapist", *Your Online Counselor,* 2007 http://youronlinecounselor.com/Articles/finding-good-therapist.htm

www.ingramcontent.com/pod-product-compliance
Lightning Source LLC
Chambersburg PA
CBHW071003160426
43193CB00012B/1895